Praise for *Changemakers*

Lots of us would like to stop global warming and endless war, end poverty, save the environment, etc. But none of us seem able to get it done. What can we do? Weller and Wilson show that we can change ourselves: how we live, what we eat, where we gather, how we interact. And out of many little personal changes may come bigger changes— within our families, communities, and the world beyond—leading to different, better outcomes.

— Dmitry Orlov, author, *Shrinking the Technosphere*

Fay Weller and Mary Wilson have written an inspiring book about how individuals can take actions that lead to transformative social change. From the first rousing story about Anna and her efforts to deal with an inane restriction on selling fresh eggs, to a description of how personal change occurs, through a wide-ranging collection of personal stories about people taking action in their communities, this is a stimulating book about how all of us can contribute to compassionate and positive change.

— Peter Robinson, former CEO of the David Suzuki Foundation

Changemakers is an accessible call to action for everyone. If we're going to find ourselves out of the ecological cul-de-sac that we find ourselves in, this is one more call to mobilize everyday life.

— Am Johal, Director,
SFU's Vancity Office of Community Engagement,
SFU Woodward's Cultural Unit

In turbulent times, we need threads of hope from which to weave our convictions into actions. If you want a guide to such action, one that is hopeful, inspiring, and practical, look no further. You have found it.

— Dan Pratt, 3M National Teaching Fellow,
Professor Emeritus & Senior Scholar,
Centre for Health Education Scholarship,
Faculty of Medicine, University of British Columbia

This is a book that traces the path from here to there: from the individual to the wider world and from the noxiousness of the present to the possibilities of the future. It does so through the stories of people in island communities who make small changes with big implications.

— Warren Magnusson, author,
Local Self-Government and the Right to the City,
Politics of Urbanism, and *The Search for Political Space*

Changemakers

Changemakers

embracing hope,
taking action, and
transforming
the world

Fay Weller and Mary Wilson

new society
PUBLISHERS

Cover design by Diane McIntosh.
Cover image © iStock (455586275).

Printed in Canada. First printing May, 2018.

This book is intended to be educational and informative. It is not intended
to serve as a guide. The author and publisher disclaim all responsibility
for any liability, loss, or risk that may be associated with the application
of any of the contents of this book.

Inquiries regarding requests to reprint all or part of *Changemakers*
should be addressed to New Society Publishers at the address below.
To order directly from the publishers, please call toll-free (North America)
1-800-567-6772 or order online at www.newsociety.com

Any other inquiries can be directed by mail to

New Society Publishers
P.O. Box 189, Gabriola Island, BC V0R 1X0, Canada
(250) 247-9737

LIBRARY AND ARCHIVES CANADA CATALOGUING IN PUBLICATION

Weller, Fay, 1958–, author

Changemakers : embracing hope, taking action, and transforming the
world / Fay Weller and Mary Wilson.

Includes bibliographical references and index.
Issued in print and electronic formats.
ISBN 978-0-86571-875-3 (softcover). — ISBN 978-1-55092-668-2 (PDF). —
ISBN 978-1-77142-263-5 (EPUB).

1. Sustainable living. 2. Human ecology. 3. Social ecology. 4. Social
change. 5. Transformative learning. I. Wilson, Mary, 1958–, author.
II. Title.

GE196.W45 2018   640.28'6   C2018-901327-3
                                          C2018-901328-1

Funded by the Government of Canada   Financé par le gouvernement du Canada

Canada

New Society Publishers' mission is to publish books that contribute
in fundamental ways to building an ecologically sustainable and
just society, and to do so with the least possible impact on the
environment, in a manner that models this vision.

Contents

SECTION C: CHANGEMAKERS' MANUAL

Preface

Where are we going?
And what am I doing in this handbasket?
—A FAVORITE FRIDGE MAGNET SAYING

Our world seems beset by crises. For us, climate change is the defining issue of our time—but we know many intelligent people who point to the refugee crisis, war, poverty, human rights atrocities, pollution of all sorts, and the ongoing struggle against totalitarianism as *the* primary problem we all face. And although this is an exhausting list, it is not an exhaustive one.

Even if we don't feel like we're all going to hell in a handbasket, it is easy to feel despair in the face of these vast, interlocking problems.

We began this book because we were looking for reasons to choose hope over despair. We find these reasons in the stories of transformation and learning that we share here, and in the idea of transformational learning as a way of moving through the crises that surround us.

What we have realized is that neither hope nor despair is sufficient, and neither is entirely relevant. Both hope and despair are emotions that are focused on the future rather than the present. The process of building a society that is based on compassion and care for the Earth and all its beings, human and otherwise, is not something that can happen only in the future. It can and must happen now. And, fortunately, for the sake of our collective future well-being, it *is* happening now. In this book, we explore the stories and experiences of individuals who are living as if the world is changing into that compassionate and caring society and, by so doing, are changing the world.

In exploring these people's stories, we are not advocating a response to climate change or any of the other issues that stop with the personal; what we are advocating is an acknowledgement of the central importance of personal change and learning in changing our world. Because all changes are initiated by people—be they individual, community, corporate, or broader changes—all change is, in part, personal change. The people we write about here have found ways to maintain hope while acknowledging despair, and to build lives based on integrity and concern for the Earth and its inhabitants. As they have done this, they have begun to challenge and change the stories and structures that support the world as it is—and perhaps change other people's stories as well.

We are writing from Canada's Gulf Islands, and many of the stories we share come from the Gulf Islands too. We are located in the southwest corner of British Columbia, just north of the San Juan Islands in the United States of America. However, while the majority of stories are from the islands, they could happen anywhere. They are tales of ordinary people embracing hope, taking action, and transforming the world.

We start our book with a section we call Changemaking, beginning with a story about eggs. In the second chapter, we talk about transformation—what we mean by it and how it comes about. The third chapter talks about ways we learn. In the fourth chapter, we discuss how transformation and learning can come together to create value-driven change at the individual, community, and societal levels. In Section B, Stories and Reflections, we hear from people as they tell their stories of transformation. We hear how change has happened through people's experiences with food, shelter, transportation, waste, energy, and economics. Each chapter is introduced with a quick overview of the issue addressed in various ways in the stories. The stories are followed by our reflections. The final chapter in this section provides a discussion about the path forward. The book closes out with our Changemakers' Manual, proposed as a guidebook for anyone, anywhere who wants to be part of co-creating a new society.

Changemaking

A Tale of Egg and Agency

If you control food you control people

On May 24, 2008 on Gabriola Island, one of the small Gulf Islands off the west coast of Canada, Anna Bauer was serving local eggs in the kitchen at the Gabriola Farmers Market. Anna was handed an official notice by the health inspector, informing her she could use only eggs that had been officially graded. She refused.

Anna describes herself as someone who would rather dig ditches than pose for pictures. She doesn't own a television set; her primary mode of transportation is her bike; and she is a member of Gabriolans for Local Food Choices, an advocacy group dedicated to seed saving, supporting local farmers, and other strategies to increase local food sovereignty.

"It's not just about eggs; they are like the canary in the mine shaft," she told the *Sounder*, Gabriola's local weekly newspaper. "We are losing ground in our accessibility to food, as well as our independence and self-sufficiency." Quoting Henry Kissinger, she said, "If you control oil you control nations, if you control food you control people," adding, "This is about control, not health."

The story from Anna's perspective:

So when this started it was in my seventh year of doing the Agi Hall [farmers market] kitchen, and until then I had not been bothered by anybody. I would just use local ingredients if I could get them...you know, as much as I could. And then this inspector showed up and told me that everything I used had to be bought...from official places, not farm gate, nothing like that, and I thought uh, huh. I said, "That includes eggs?"...Oh, yeah.

So, anyways, I told him that I would not oblige him with that and he could choose to be warned...because I understood that he had a discretionary clause and he didn't have to do everything to the letter. I understood that someone with his job would have that—they don't have to be antagonistic.

He responded...in an extreme way, and he said as long as he had that job there was no way that he could ignore that, because of the health risks. So then I said, "You must know that the health risks are worse on the other side," but he couldn't go there. He urged me to respect the regulations, and I said no way—he chose the wrong person to do that battle. He wasn't going to get any concession from me. I just wanted to be clear about that—I didn't want to lie about it.

It's almost possible to feel sympathy for the inspector; he had certainly chosen to challenge someone who was up to the challenge. Anna knew a lot about the difference between the eggs laid by local chickens and those which, while inspected, mostly likely came from factory farms. She saw a clear connection between the regulations on egg grading and larger, systemic issues, and she was sure she had the right to say no. So she did.

Because of that I couldn't get a permit, which was used against me. Without the permit to run the kitchen, which I'd never needed before, all of a sudden I had to pay a fee of $120 to get the permit. But I could only get the permit if everything came from official sources—it circled. So I chose to operate without the permit. I told the Agi board and they accepted me and they said, "Do it, do whatever."

Anna used local self-governance, in the form of the local community group that ran the farmers market, to resist the inspector's use of permits as an enforcement tool. Because the Agriculture Hall Board (Agi Board) supported her rationale for using local uninspected free-range eggs, they were willing to stand up against the government's security measures.

Gabriola is a small island, and the story spread rapidly. When the health inspector arrived at the farmers market with a letter aimed at shutting Anna down, some fellow islanders showed up in the kitchen in support of Anna.

> *I think in the end there were seven people there. And so he told me—he ordered me—to shut down the operation. So I said, "Okay, I won't oblige. What's the next step?" So he told me the next step was a warning, and there were four stages with the final one being, you know, not the police but the equivalent, a few heavy-handed men would come...and I said, "Okay, I'll go with that because that will be really good PR,"...and I said, "I don't mind."*

Anna exercised her free will, and having others around her provided support for that position. In the health inspector's mind Anna was a subject of the government and he, as a representative of that government, was there to ensure she complied with the public good, as determined by the government. By exercising her internal authority, backed by friends supporting her position, she was challenging the health inspector's story about who the defender of the public good was.

> *So, then he got really upset and shoved me. And at that point Jenny said, "Take your hands off her—that is assault". But he was also heavy handed with Signe who was taking pictures of that—and he pushed her too—so he had completely lost it.*

The health inspector's response indicates his anger, frustration, and bewilderment at not being acknowledged and respected as the official authority on public health—an authority to be feared, since from his perspective he wielded the power to close the business. His story was based on a belief in the "rightness" of the regulations that he was enforcing. He knew his job. The government's aim was to prevent salmonella, and according to his story he was representing *the* public health solution. Anna's story was different. Anna and the seven people gathered in the kitchen in support of her stance did not believe that his actions promoted better public health; they recognized Anna as the authority in this interaction, not the health inspector.

The dynamic between Anna and the health inspector expanded to a challenge from the island community to the Vancouver Island Health Authority (VIHA) regarding best practices in public health:

> There was a petition—a lot of people signed. A potluck was organized because during that time we also discovered that public potlucks were illegal. You cannot just invite the public—you have to have a food safety plan and all that. So we did that as a protest. And it was very well attended.

Over 300 people signed the petition, and 150 people protested the egg and potluck regulations.

The challenge became a news item that quickly spread from local to national media:

> Someone had called [the editor of the local paper] so she came, but she came after all that had happened and made the news. And then it just kind of went from one thing to another—it made national news without me doing anything.
>
> Some of the people I had as regular customers were connected to CBC [Canadian public radio and television], especially one—he and his wife came every single Saturday. Shelagh Rogers [a nationally known CBC host] also came occasionally, and Shelagh's husband was also a regular. So, if it wasn't for them I don't think it would have gone viral...so, it was just one of the lucky coincidences I think.

Anna Bauer was invited onto the CBC and featured in news media across Canada; all critiqued the government's policy. Apparently, her beliefs about food safety are echoed by many others across Canada. Two years after Anna refused to comply with the health inspector's demands, the health authority changed its policy, and uninspected farm fresh eggs can now be sold in restaurants and grocery stores. Local food advocates held celebrations throughout the region!

When the health inspector handed Anna that official notice, she was at the receiving end of a well-intentioned government objective. In the case of the uninspected eggs, the government's aim was to reduce the incidence of salmonella contamination, a goal that is hard to argue with. The approaches used to reduce salmonella include regulations requiring official inspection and the grading of all eggs sold to the public, enforcement in the form of health inspectors and fines to ensure implementation of the regulations, and the language to provide the official rationale used for public consumption.

The truth at the heart of the government's story is the dangers of salmonella, and the government's duty to safeguard public health. But this truth is not complete, and the story doesn't cover all circumstances. The government's rationale for the problem of salmonella is based on records of food contaminated by food handlers and problems with ungraded eggs. It doesn't include the research that found five times more incidences of salmonella in battery egg operations relative to organic farms or the study that found that reducing the use of antimicrobials in poultry reduced the incidence of salmonella. The regulations are designed to address the problem the official story tells us about but nothing else.

When the mainstream media cover issues like this, voices representing corporate interest (such as the BC Egg Marketing Board) rather than public interest often find their way into the stories. The following quote is from the *Nanaimo Daily News* (February 17, 2009):

> **When is Produce Safe to Buy?**
> *Restaurants and grocery stores can now sell ungraded, farm-fresh eggs after a policy change by the Vancouver Island Health Authority, but businesses that choose to do so could be putting the public at undue risk, warns the B.C. Egg Marketing Board.*

The change to health authority policy highlights the potential for questioning the status quo and shifting policy, even in the face of strong government and corporate interests. Anna's support from the island community, the media's interest in a farmers market story in the middle of summer, and the resulting outpouring of public opinion across the country redefined the story-telling space. It was no longer the action of a single health inspector against a single food services vendor; the space was expanded to include a broader discussion and opportunities to learn different stories about food safety and its definition. Repealing the rule that prevented Anna from selling uninspected eggs at a local farmers market is part of a broader shift towards different stories about food and public health.

Anna gives us plenty to consider as we start on the pathway towards hope, and the desire to co-create a compassionate world. In the next three chapters, we will let Anna's story shine a light on how each of us can become part of that co-creation.

Transformation

Personal transformation is the starting point for societal transformation, and it occurs when our stories about ourselves and the world change. How does this happen? Anna provides us with some insights. We must want to live a life of integrity, be ready to hear different stories, and be open to learning from these stories. From these factors transformational learning arises. Dots are connected. And we move into alignment with our values, holding a new understanding of ourselves and the world.

Integrity

Integrity means being whole or undivided—when our actions and words are consistent with our core values and beliefs, we live a life of integrity. Anna epitomizes the word *integrity*. She could not fathom serving eggs that were not produced in a way that was consistent with her values. The diagram depicts a circle with a 'V' (for values) and

Integrity

a corresponding 'A' (for actions). Integrity arises when Values and Actions are aligned, as depicted in the whole circle.

The desire to create actions that correspond to our values is central to the idea of transformation. To live lives of integrity we must be aware of our own values—actions cannot deliberately be consistent with values that are not really understood. What is evident in the egg story is that Anna is very clear on her values, and her clarity allows her to follow a definitive course of action.

The practice of integrity leads naturally to the practice of self-reflection, since integrity requires an honest and critical look at personal values and assumptions. If we want to live a life of integrity, our values and actions need to be aligned. Our inner voice will let us know when they misalign.

Shifting stories

Transformation is not a tinkering at the edges but rather a complete change to a different mode of thinking and being. How does this happen? We think of it as a radical shift in perspective— a sometimes sudden realization that the things we thought we believed no longer really represent our understanding. We think of this as a shift of stories.

As human beings, we build our world through our stories. In his book *The Storytelling Animal: How Stories Make Us Human*, Jonathan Gottschall expresses this powerfully:

> *Only humans tell stories. Story sets us apart. For humans, story is like gravity: a field of force that surrounds us and influences all of our movements. But, like gravity, story is so omnipresent that we are hardly aware of how it shapes our lives.*

We live in a society that, like all societies, tells powerful stories about how the world should be and how we should be in the world. Transformation requires us to become aware of those stories, see them for what they are, and replace them with other tales of how both we and the world can be. The reassessment of societal stories, and the process of seeing and understanding a different story that is based on mindfulness and integrity, is similar to the experience of always seeing the candlestick in the diagram and then suddenly seeing the faces (or visa versa).

Anna's experience is a clear example of two different stories in the same space: one, Anna's experience of the superiority of farm fresh eggs, and the other, that the official version of inspected eggs equals healthy population. Anna was able to clearly see both stories due to her values and her desire to live with integrity.

Although we are writing about radical personal transformation, this process of reassessment does not mean throwing everything out without reflection and just starting all over. After all, the things we saw originally are usually still there, and as much as we may change our minds and way of living, we are still the same people. Instead it means being first aware of, and then reflective about, the stories we hear, attempting to understand where they come from, what they attempt to explain, and who that explanation benefits.

Who benefits from the egg regulations? The regulations around the grading of eggs were created to respond to the issues faced by large factory chicken farms, not by backyard free-ranging chickens. The British Columbia Egg Marketing Board (BCEMB) represents the interests of its members, registered egg producers averaging 17,000 chickens per farm. In 1967, the BCEMB was given the mandate to "promote, control, and regulate the production, transportation, packing, storage, and marketing of all eggs in British Columbia, including the prohibition of all or part of these activities." It created the egg inspection regulation in response to salmonella found in factory eggs, and that's the story that collided with Anna's insistence on serving locally raised eggs.

The requirement for all eggs to be inspected works for the large factory chicken farms but makes no sense for eggs from small local farms. The cost is prohibitive to take a few eggs in to an inspection facility and then back home again. The acknowledgement that eggs from pasture-fed chickens are healthier than those being inspected doesn't enter into the official story, and thus it doesn't enter into the regulations either.

The reflective reassessment process may call on us to dig deep into history, gradually coming to see the roots of a story for what it is, as demonstrated in the history behind the egg regulations. Or it may be that we immediately recognize a story that is blatantly incongruent with our values and reality and is ripe for replacement. Anna's response was immediate due to her clarity about her values and her knowledge about healthy eggs, but others may need to look more deeply to understand the origins of the different stories. Sometimes we may recognize some value within the story and use that portion to build a new story that is not harmful to the Earth or other living creatures.

This may sound like a pleasant activity—quiet storytelling for a winter's afternoon. We see it as much more urgent. We live on a planet that is being reshaped by climate change—climate change that we as people are causing. It is a world where literally millions of people (65 million as of 2016) have become refugees, forced from their homes by myriad political crises and natural disasters. It is a world rife with inequalities of all sorts. It is crucial that we understand when societal stories are leading us closer to disaster and what new stories could lead us on another path.

Transformative spaces

Personal transformation starts with being in a space that offers opportunities for us to hear new stories about ourselves and the world around us. These spaces can be anywhere—in our homes, our communities, our workplaces, or elsewhere in the wider world. They may be spaces we spend time in frequently or spaces that we visit very infrequently or only virtually. The nature of the space is not what is important; what is important is that the space "makes space" for new stories.

The kitchen at the farmers market was a transformative space—it provided space for more than

Transformative Space

one story about healthy eggs, and it also provided two stories about authority. Those in the kitchen and those witnessing the discussion had the opportunity to hear all these stories.

We may discover these stories and analyze them in different ways. Sometimes we find them purely through the process of reflection that we've already talked about. Sometimes we encounter them in a different way. We see someone else who has chosen a different path and seems to be acting from an entirely different basis. When that person shares their stories, we may be challenged to think about our own.

These spaces may feel distressing and discordant. We might experience what has been called a "disorienting dilemma"— a feeling that a new story seems to be true yet contradicts a long-cherished personal belief. The spaces may feel wonderful—places where we suddenly feel that we have found somewhere to belong. We may sometimes experience both sensations almost simultaneously. The sensations of dissonance come from a deep understanding that the societal story that we have learned does not fit with our reality or experience. The resonance comes from seeing the possibility of a new story that is integral to our core values.

We can easily envision one of the seven people in that farmer's kitchen experiencing both a disorienting dilemma, as they discovered that the public health system isn't always the protector of our health, and a resonance with Anna's values and her willingness to stand up for her beliefs.

Some of the stories in this book will identify that kind of sudden dilemma and its aftermath. Other storytellers we listened to found, in the slow accumulation of information and experiences, a growing realization of the dissonance between societal stories and their own core values and beliefs. Many mentioned key moments of resonance in which they felt at one with the Earth and recognized the need for a different way of being in the world, for the Earth's sake as well as their own.

Transformative spaces are important, but they are not enough. The deconstruction and reconstruction of societal stories happens only when we as listeners are ready to become aware of different stories. That readiness involves openness, a desire for integrity, and a kind of personal courage. We see three components to this courage: willingness to let go of what will be lost if a story is abandoned, willingness to allow multiple realities, and willingness to truly hear stories from multiple perspectives. It's really an iterative process. We cultivate our courage through reflection on our values and through a longing for integrity in all areas of our lives. At the same time, reflection on our values gives us the courage to make changes.

We hold on to stories because they give us something—a direct benefit, protection from fear—or one of a dozen other reasons. The benefit can be an image of ourselves that we want to hold on to, a competing value, or a pleasure that we don't want to give up. As an example, think about food. Organic and local products can often be more expensive than mass-produced food. If we are holding on to a "get the best deal" story drummed into us as children, we continue buying the mass-produced food or the factory-farmed egg, even though we suspect a difference in health and environmental results. When we open ourselves up to hearing different stories, we must understand any resistance we have to that story in light of what we might lose. Our analytical mind works hand in hand with our values to support actions that stem from those values rather than old stories.

Every moment holds multiple realities. Picture a park with some people picnicking and others kicking a ball. A raccoon skitters through the trees, and a bird lands on a branch nearby the picnickers. Each of the people—the bird, the raccoon, those playing ball, and the trees themselves—experience a different reality of that same moment. Once we recognize the multiple realities, then it becomes easier to hear and understand stories that are different from our own, and different from those societal stories we thought were universal. This recognition is the starting point for compassion.

What were the different realities at the farmers market? The health inspector, Anna, Signe, Jenny, the customers, and the newspaper editor all experienced Anna's free will event differently. All their stories are relevant when understanding how change happens.

If we spend time with only like-minded people, we are not likely to hear stories that are unfamiliar. If we don't have a chance to hear the myriad stories that are told about our world, it doesn't matter that we're willing to listen to them. The world is full of activities and of people who have very different perspectives from our own—no matter what our own perspectives may be. Seeking out difference and exercising curiosity will give us a chance to hear the many, many stories the world has to tell us and to learn that our stories, too, are just stories. If you are reading this book then you are already interested in making change happen. Engage with those who don't want the same change that you do. What stories do they believe and why? Meeting others where they are gives you the chance to see their practices, reflect on their relevance for your own life, and think about how their stories can inform yours.

Free will: engaging our capacity to act

The idea that our every action is predetermined, or that our choices are entirely controlled by global forces beyond our control, are themselves stories. In the previous section, we talked about the willingness to change. Our will—our acknowledgement that we do have choices—is central to this.

Free Will

We have a choice about whether or not we want to live the way societal stories tell us to or live in a way that feels integral to our values and the new stories that we are constructing. We have depicted the concept of free will with a sign post showing that we have many different choices for the way we live our life.

Anna is a shining example of living life according to one's values and choosing to live by the stories she believed. This choice starts with believing we have a right to question the assumptions that underlie all of the stories we hear. Is capitalism the only type of economy? Why do we need countries? Why does a large house symbolize success? When we question the assumptions behind these ideas, we open ourselves to new stories.

We also have the right, through our free will, to question laws and regulations that feel contrary to our values. Again, Anna provides us with a great example of questioning laws and regulations. Recognition of our free will sets us free to acknowledge that, while governments may believe they have ultimate authority over us, they don't. Anna proved that we can challenge government and overturn unjust policies. Governments have laws, regulations, and enforcement mechanisms to make us follow those laws. But we have the choice of standing up for what we believe.

Another aspect of free will is recognizing how much choice we have in our everyday life to live life according to our beliefs, our values, our own transformed societal stories. The majority of actions and behaviors don't involve any form of government. We can grow food in our garden (backyard or community plot); we can swap clothes with others or buy them at a thrift store; and we can ride our bikes, walk, or take the bus rather than driving. Our free will allows us to make our own lifestyle choices—and our ability to recognize multiple stories helps us understand and smile at criticisms of our unusual choices. At the same time, our choices can make it more possible for others we know to make new choices. By sharing our stories with the world—whether explicitly or just through our daily actions—we are adding to the collection of stories that others experience.

Experiencing a transformative shift in a societal story is not one single incident but rather a lifelong process. The first time you are consciously aware of a shift is the start of many more shifts. The awareness that the world is not as you assumed, and that the role you play in the world is also not what you assumed, opens your mind and heart to hearing and feeling other stories. Learning about these new stories occurs in many ways—through compassion, through critical reflection, and through mindful practice. These ways of learning/being are intertwined and complementary.

We will talk about these ways of learning in Chapter 3.

Learning Change

Change is the end result of all true learning.

—LEO BUSCAGLIA

Learning is the process by which we change our minds and then come to align our actions in the world with our new views. It is fundamental to the kind of transformations we are talking about in this book. In the stories we share, you will find examples of people changing their minds and learning new ways of doing things. Our focus is on transforming the world in a way that is better for people and for the planet. It's easy to make that sound as if we think learning is an unmitigated good—always a wonderful step towards liberation. It is not. We are sadly aware that learning is not always positive. We can all point to many, many examples of people who have learned that they are somehow less valuable than others; the schools of racism, sexism, homophobia and all kinds of oppression teach their brutal lessons well. These stories of "less than," "not good enough," and "not worthy" are all too frequently given voice. By our focus on the positive we do not mean to deny the existence of the negative.

When we talk about learning, we're thinking beyond dictionary definitions that describe it as the process of gaining knowledge or skills through instruction, experience, or observation. We see it as the way in which we come to live in the way we do.

Although our definition is broader than most, we find some value in the way educators describe learning processes. In the world of education, teachers often think of learning as one of three types: cognitive, psychomotor, or affective. We think of these three as the learning of the head, the hand, and the heart. All of them are important to the process of personal transformation and social change.

Learning in the cognitive domain, learning in the head, is what many of us remember from school—sonnets and quadratic equations, the distance from the Earth to the Sun, and the date of the French revolution. All those facts that can be remembered or Googled—all that "book learning"—fits within the cognitive domain. So too do the critical thinking skills that are so important for challenging society's familiar stories: the ability to question assumptions, look for benefits, and recognize dissonance are all part of this domain.

The physical skills—keyboarding, shooting a basketball, tying a bowline—are skills of the psychomotor domain. Of course, these "doing" things require thinking as well, but there comes a time when the body seems to know how to do what the mind no longer needs to consciously think about. This domain is sometimes the subject of "lesser than" stories—work in the trades is typically seen as less important than more intellectual work, for example, although this story is changing.

The third domain, the affective domain, is the domain of emotion and attitude—the domain where we learn to value some things above others. The affective domain is where stories have their power. The cautionary tale, the terrible example—all those stories of people who have strayed from their expected societal path or, in other circles, taken up a traditional role and returned to the societal fold—those stories work in the affective domain. We learn that individuals in certain groups are inferior or dangerous, not typically through rational study or evaluation of data, but through stories.

Most ideas about learning are metaphors—different ways of visualizing a process that is complex and individual. Even the seemingly simple separation of cognitive, psychomotor, and affective domains of learning is no more than metaphorical. After all, each of these types of learning involves thinking; each involves an emotional reaction or connection; each takes place in our human body. Since they are all metaphorical, it's worth finding a metaphor that works. For us, it is easiest to think of the types of learning as embodied characters, and for that we have turned to the Buddhist metaphor of the bodhisattva.

Bodhisattvas are interesting characters. In Buddhist art, they are often depicted in fantastic ways—human figures with many eyes and arms, great warriors with huge flaming swords. They're not supernatural, though. Instead, they are archetypes that represent the best of human intention and character. There are many bodhisattvas (fortunately, since we all need lots of help), but there are three that are especially good metaphors for the learning that changes the world. The three we'll talk about represent wisdom (Manjushri), compassion (Avalokiteśvara) and practice (Samantabhadra).

The names themselves are not so very important. What is important is the recognition that these are old names and old ideas. People have been exploring this way of thinking about intention, change, and the significance of our actions in the world for a very long time.

Learning through critical reflection: wielding the sword of wisdom

Let's start with Manjushri, a fierce-looking individual who holds up a flaming sword. The sword represents wisdom and the ability to cut through nonsense and see things accurately. There's a clear connection here with the idea of cognitive learning, and especially to the kind of sudden new understanding that transforms a worldview. If a seemingly immutable truth is to be challenged, and overturned, Manjushri is likely the one challenging it.

It's this kind of certainty of wisdom and clear vision that lets someone like Anna stand up to something like a regulation that seems, in her wisdom, to be invalid. Anna had knowledge. She

knew what the regulations were designed for, but more importantly she understood why they had been developed. She was
convinced that her knowledge of the safety practices
of local farmers—the knowledge inherent in her
knowledge of her community—was more important
for food safety in her kitchen than government regulations designed by and for large egg-producers.
As she made her fried-egg sandwiches she wielded
that knowledge like a sword (or in this case, perhaps,
like a spatula).

Egg of
Wisdom

There are many other examples of the wisdom of
Manjushri in action, and often on a larger scale. Well-
known climate activists like Al Gore (with *An Incon-
venient Truth*) and Bill McKibben (*The End of Nature*,
and 350.org), by clearly and simply stating what is
happening to the world's climate, have shocked many
people into a knowledge of human-caused climate
change. Activists in Black Lives Matter point out the
astonishing number of black youth killed by police, and this fact
enters our consciousness. All kinds of awareness campaigns attempt to use the sword of wisdom to enlighten the rest of us, making it impossible for us to say that we didn't know.

This archetype also represents critical reflection. This type of
learning is about questioning societal myths and seeking to understand both the myth's source as well as other ways of understanding the topic at the heart of the myth. As Doris Lessing said,
"That is what learning is. You suddenly understand something
you've understood all your life, but in a new way." Using the egg
example again, as someone just reading about the story of Anna
and the egg, you might be suddenly struck by the knowledge that
industry lobbyists have something to do with the setting of government safety regulations. This may be an entirely new realization. You might begin by thinking about eggs and then realize
that there are other instances—in other aspects of food safety, in
pharmaceuticals, and in a host of other places—where governments make regulations. You might be challenged by this initial

thought to really investigate how regulations are developed, and even to think about the wisdom of uncritically following them. When the sword cuts, it can cut deeply.

Learning the Manjushri way involves willingness to question both the stories and priorities found in our communities and the broader society. Elgin Isin describes this type of learning as that moment when "the naturalness of the dominant virtues is called into question and their arbitrariness revealed." Once something that has seemed like an everyday truth is revealed as something arbitrary, it's natural to consider why the story was created, who benefits from it, and who suffers. As we work to answer these questions, we learn. As we learn, we observe the impact these stories have on us—or on others besides us.

What does the egg story show us about learning? In this story, it is Anna who is in the role of Manjushri—the bringer of wisdom and the challenger of accepted truth. About 150 islanders attended the illegal egg potluck; it's safe to assume that many of them would have taken up the egg of wisdom with Anna from the start, but very likely others were prompted by her action to examine their own beliefs and discover the disjunction between the goal of health inspection (keeping us safe) and its implementation (keeping us from consuming something that is safer than the inspected product). And even if every single Gabriolan was already a supporter and consumer of uninspected, farm-raised eggs—unlikely to say the least—Anna's message spread across the country via the media. We can never know how many people learned to question the food safety system and its impact on local food producers based on her actions; nor can we know the improvements to the food safety system that could result.

When we start to understand that a story is just that—one story that can be told about the world and how it works—we may also start to explore alternatives. This type of learning links critical reflection with mindful everyday living as we become conscious of a different way of understanding a particular aspect of the world and, as a result, we behave in a way that corresponds to that new understanding.

Learning through compassion: hearing the cries of the world

The sudden shock of new knowledge is one way to prompt a change of perspective, but it is not the only one. Another way is through an upwelling of compassion: the deep understanding of another's position and point of view.

Avalokiteśvara, the bodhisattva who represents compassion is usually shown with many arms, ears, and eyes—to hear and see the suffering of the world and offer consolation. The number of arms, eyes, and ears varies depending on the geographical location of the artist. So does gender; Avalokiteśvara is sometimes male and sometimes female. The role stays the same, though.

As a word, *compassion* is formed from the roots *co* (together) and *passion*. Being compassionate involves feeling what others are experiencing, and being moved to take some action. Compassion isn't pity. Feeling is the beginning, but wise action is also part of it. This is the image of Avalokiteśvara, with a hundred eyes and ears to see and hear, and a hundred arms to help. Empathy matters here too. Empathy, placing or imagining ourselves in another's place, is core to transformative learning. Empathy requires us to acknowledge other realities. When we think back to the picnickers, birds, trees, and ball players we talked about earlier, we can understand that each being experienced that moment differently. Each being also had a different history leading up to that moment and will have a different future. One of the ball players may have come from a war-torn country in Africa, while another may have been born to wealthy North American parents. The bird may have flown from across the continent as part of its migration path, and the tree may be over 100 years old and have witnessed the change from a forest to a park. If something happened to disturb that park—for example, if development was planned or if there was a sudden upsurge in violence directed against one of the ball players—our sense of empathy with the enjoyment that all were experiencing in the park might prompt us to act.

One definition of compassion from the Buddhist tradition is "solidarity of the heart." When we are in solidarity with others, we take their struggles for our own. We feel a deep connection with the object of our compassion, be it a human being or another creature. There is no element of pity in this view of compassion; instead, there is a strong and powerful sense of identification and an experience of another perspective.

When we learn from a place of compassion, we understand the reality of the person across from us at a community meeting; we pay attention to the seedling struggling with lack of water; we research the working conditions of those making a product we want to purchase. Compassion can be seen in the person who uses wind and water power to provide electricity, watching for signs in the environment that tell him or her how to adjust their energy systems to produce the electricity they need. Being side by side with the environment or another person provides the opportunity for understanding, but the closeness does not automatically result in that understanding. We must be willing to listen, to watch, to ask questions, to observe; we must be willing to understand what it would be like to "walk a mile in their shoes."

The practice of compassion is a practice of openness, of being willing to work hard not only to understand another's perspective but to share it as one possibility in a range of possibilities—as one story that has as much value as our own.

We see compassionate action and compassionate teachers at work in the world every day. Environmentalists like Jane Goodall encourage us to extend our compassion beyond the human world; advocates for oppressed people everywhere also push us to identify with others. Compassion doesn't just give rise to fuzzy warm feelings. If we extend a compassionate gaze to the situation at the farmers market, we'll see that there were many more people involved than just Anna and the inspector. Her friends and supporters stood by her. It's easy to feel their compassion—their sense that it can be difficult to stand up alone and that support is helpful. Looking around the market, though, there are others to consider—the small farmers whose sale of eggs can be an important part of their income; the individual with a compromised immune system who might be particularly concerned about food safety and relying on the government's inspection system to ensure it; the chickens laying the eggs, in most cases enjoying an outdoor life and free-range pasture; and the inspector himself, committed to the defense of regulations and the safety of the community. Compassion won't bring us to agree with everyone, but it does help us see their perspectives.

Learning through mindful practice: taking action in the world

We've talked about the learning of the heart through compassion, and of the head through the development of wisdom. The third kind of learning is the learning of the hand. The bodhisattva Samantabhadra is one metaphor for this type of learning. While Manjushri represents awareness/wisdom and Avalokiteśvara represents compassion, Samantabhadra represents compassion and awareness coming together in action.

Images of Samantabhadra aren't quite as consistent as the images of flaming sword and multiple hands we've been talking about. Samantabhadra is usually shown doing something—sometimes waving a lotus blossom, sometimes resisting temptation of various sorts, sometimes playing a musical instrument. Most of the images are images of something being done with care. This is the image of mindful practice.

Mindful practice is about moment-to-moment action, informed by compassion and wisdom. It is about integrity and doing—a "hand" approach to learning. There are three aspects to this type of learning. There is learning by doing itself, and there is learning through watching others and then following their example. A third aspect draws from the underlying reason for learning—to live life in a way that benefits all living beings as we move through the world.

Aristotle spoke to the first aspect of "hand" learning in *The Nicomachean Ethics*: "For the things we have to learn before we can do them, we learn by doing them." If we are growing our own food we can read about best practices and watch instructional videos on the internet, but until we plant the seed, nurture it, watch it grow, harvest it, and consume it, then we haven't fully learned how to grow food. Benjamin Franklin speaks to the learning that comes only from experience: "Tell me and I forget, teach me and I may remember, involve me and I learn."

The second aspect of learning through mindful practice arises when we witness ways of being and doing. As children, we learn our language and our way of being in the world from our parents and other family members. Just as we learn language from being around our parents, we learn certain practices when we venture into cultures that differ from those we grew up in. We might find different cultural norms in organizations or the broader community. When we see Anna standing up to the imposition of rules she feels are unjust, we learn that it is possible to step outside the world of unquestioned authority. The learning may involve mindfulness and our own sense of compassion—for example, we recognize the environmental and human rights implications when buying thrift store clothes rather than new clothes made overseas. Or the learning may be aimed at another objective—we do it to fit in with those around us. We may also do it because we see traits we admire, whether in a human or another creature:

A person can learn a lot from a dog, even a loopy one like ours. Marley taught me about living each day with unbridled exuberance and joy, about seizing the moment and following your heart. He taught me to appreciate the simple things—a walk in the woods, a fresh snowfall, a nap in a shaft of winter sunlight. And as he grew old and achy, he taught me about optimism in the face of adversity. Mostly, he taught me about friendship and selflessness and, above all else, unwavering loyalty.

—JOHN GROGAN, *Marley and Me:*
Life and Love with the World's Worst Dog

There are so many examples of mindful practice for us to see in the world that it's not difficult to think of an example. Think of someone that you know who seems to embody their wisdom and care for the world in the way they live.

Wisdom, compassion, and practice: making connections

Many of the stories of success that we've heard in our culture—the value of individualism, ownership, and the importance of winning, among others—work, most obviously, against the practice of compassion. They also make it difficult to notice and value the practices of others—the stories tell us that, rather than admiring integrity in action, we should envy accomplishments, reputation, and possessions. Shifting away from such practices, when they have been promoted as societal values, is a challenge that requires continual awareness. It is difficult, if not impossible, to be compassionate towards the environment and others, or to choose to emulate them, if there is no desire to understand their context and stories but focus instead is on being right, winning, or gaining ownership.

What is missing in the story of individualism is that we are all connected, as organisms on this Earth, like a giant three-dimensional weaving. In the Buddhist tradition this weaving is called Indra's Net. In this image of the interconnection of the universe, everything—or at least every form of consciousness—exists as a jewel at a joining point of a great net. Each jewel is an individual, yet each jewel reflects all the others. The metaphor is Buddhist, but the idea is not. Albert Einstein also said that our separation from others and from nature is a delusion:

> A human being is a part of the whole called by us universe, a part limited in time and space. He experiences himself, his thoughts, and feeling as something separated from the rest, a kind of optical delusion of his consciousness. This delusion is a kind of prison for us, restricting us to our personal desires and to affection for a few persons nearest to us. Our task must be to free ourselves from

> *this prison by widening our circle of compassion to embrace all*
> *living creatures and the whole of nature in its beauty.*

The optical delusion Einstein noticed encourages us to establish "us against them" ways of interacting, operating, and governing. The multiplicity of organizations and cliques in a community creates a multitude of intents that are often at cross-purposes, and thus visceral, defensive reactions, rather than empathy, occur. It's difficult to recognize wisdom when it appears, particularly if it's being demonstrated by someone already labeled Other. Through "widening our circle of compassion" learning occurs and battles are diffused. The learning involves an increased understanding about how a proposed action may impact others and what their intents or purposes are that are different from what we had in mind and, thus, may be causing friction.

Compassion can lead to critical reflection, as we understand the lived experience of other creatures and organisms within this world. When we feel a sense of solidarity of the heart with a person working twelve hours a day side by side with hundreds of other people in an unsafe building, then we may start seeing the damage our current systems and stories are creating. Similarly, critical reflection can lead to compassion; our awareness of working conditions may prompt us to feel compassion for workers we will never meet.

The three ways of learning—represented by head, hand, and heart—are closely intertwined. We attempt to do something with mindful attention, and our thoughts turn to the "why" behind it. Through critical reflection, we examine our actions—not just critiquing our skill, or lack of it, but reflecting on the importance of what we are doing for the wider world. Why is it important to restore this old skill? Why should I spend my time learning to make something by hand, when I can purchase it cheaply? The "why" questions lead us to compassion: because we are aware of the actions we take, we also become aware of who benefits, and who is hurt, by those actions.

We return to the metaphor of the bodhisattvas and imagine that all three of these voices are within us; this is the kind of internal conversation that we experience as we learn how to engage in a societal transformation. The hand, the head, and the heart—each is a crucial element of learning how to engage in a societal transformation in a way that supports our own happiness and well-being as we participate in changing the world. Imagining these three beings helps us to think about the ongoing dance of learning and change as transformation happens.

The How of Change

From personal transformation to societal change

So far, we've been writing about individual transformation. We've talked about the ways in which transformation can begin—deconstructing societal stories, understanding multiple realities, and acting on our integrity through free will. We've talked about how change can be learned—with the analytical mind, compassion, and practical hands-on doing. Now we turn our attention to the connections between individual change and broader, societal change.

How does individual learning and transformation shift into "a small group of thoughtful, committed citizens" changing the world? We'll be looking to Anna and her network of changemakers as we explore how networks, nodes, and iterative learning, as well as the phases of change, all work to provide some insight into this question. We'll also take a look into the scary world of corporate globalization and how the relationship between local and global shines a light on the "how" of societal change.

Iterative

Does social change happen as the cumulative result of many instances of personal transformation? Does it happen when societal structures change, requiring a new response? As we have worked through these stories, we've come to see it as a "both/and" rather than an "either/or" process. The process of change is a process of learning, and we learn in many different ways. We can and do learn from the way our society is organized; as we learn new ways of living, the individual changes we make change the social structures we co-create.

Let's take a moment to look at how Anna's story sheds a light on the iterative nature of change. The starting point was Anna reaching the point of knowing that the local farm-fresh eggs she served at the farmers market were healthier than chicken-factory inspected eggs. She arrived at that point through personal transformation—an ability to see a different story from the official story.

Those around Anna learned from her and/or went through their own personal transformation to arrive at the same values and beliefs. This group, together with the media, may have influenced anyone listening to the story on the radio or reading it in the news. Due in part to the heightened media attention and public support for Anna's position, this group managed to persuade the health authority officials to change the regulations. Once the regulations had been changed, more people had the opportunity to eat uninspected local farm fresh eggs. As more people choose to buy eggs from small local farmers, that action shifts from being a rare occurrence, to an acceptable practice, and then to the preferable/mainstream one. This small group of islanders demonstrates how a net of interconnections is part of creating a cultural shift in society.

Living net

Let's go back to the concept of Indra's net and create a picture in our head—let's imagine threads linking each of us to all the direct connections that we have to other people and to the Earth. One thread could represent our next door neighbor, and another could represent the relationship between ourselves and the food we had for breakfast. Still others could represent each of the people on our street, and another thread the air that we are breathing. Let's then imagine all of those threads linking to their connections.

The thread to our breakfast food eventually links to the soil that produced it and to the farmers. The threads connecting us to our neighbors are now linked through them to others in their life. We are part of a living net.

Nodes are the places where two threads meet in the network. These are symbolized by jewels or pearls in Indra's net, and each one reflects all the others. If we are open to learning, this is where magic happens, where we can experience a different   Living Net story, one that transforms the way we understand and act in the world. As learning and personal transformation occur at a place of connection, then that is communicated back through the threads linking us to others, to our neighbors, to our community, to the world.

The threads transfer that new societal story or way of thinking to others. A thread can be the internet, a film, a book, a community gathering, a potluck dinner, art, or a song. It can be words or actions: visual, tactile, or auditory. As that new societal story becomes part of our way of seeing the world, then we start to envision or dream ways in which the society around us could be more consistent with that new story. How does change happen? It happens through dreaming the possibilities, followed by actions taken by small groups of people, as epitomized by Anna and described by Margaret Mead's well known quote: "Never doubt that a small group of thoughtful, committed citizens can change the world."

The how of change

We're going to describe the process of social change as if it were linear. In practice, however, the process will likely include elements of excitement or frustration, a sense of two steps forward and one back, or be experienced as a labyrinth or spiral rather than a straight line. Even so, let's walk through the phases one by one:

1. Personal transformation occurs. People learn a different societal story and see the possibility of a better world. Martin Luther King Junior's famous speech, "I have a dream," epitomizes this step.

2. People see the many possibilities that they can be part of, individually and with others, to make local changes happen. And they start working on making those happen. By *local* we don't just mean geographically; we also mean within your personal networks: your cousins in Phoenix or Newfoundland or Australia, your work colleagues in Italy and China, your online connections stretching throughout the world.

3. Other people and organizations may have intents or purposes that are consistent with their societal story; however, they are at cross purposes with the possibilities you (and others) have envisioned. This phase can include either visceral disagreement or and/or compassionate understanding for each other's intent and a desire to come to agreement on how to achieve both intents.

4. Parallel with stage three is the spiral or labyrinth. An idea may spark and happen right away because people around see the need, the regulations don't get in the way, and the resources are available to make it happen. However, the majority of stories in this book describe a spiral of activity as cross-purposes, regulations, or lack of information or understanding on the part of the initiators or community members that result in delays and the need for patience.

spiral

5. That local change then interconnects with other local changes. There is the possibility of the interconnected living web of change described above.

6. The shifting of threads, and the corresponding shifts of many

more threads in the living net, changes culture and starts to finally change government regulations and actions as the majority of the population demands change from governments.

Phase one has been described in the Transformation and Learning Change chapters. As a way of understanding phase two let's think of our society as a house described as a fixer upper. We walk around the house, and we see possibilities. We see the possibility of a beautiful hardwood floor under the ugly orange carpet. We see the possibility of sunlight streaming into the kitchen and dining room if a wall gets torn down. We also see the possibility of electrical malfunction when we look in the electrical panel. We have a dream of turning this fixer upper into a dream house, but we need to take that next step and actually do it.

Possibilities arise from our imaginations and from our dreams of a better world. If we can imagine what the world looks like in our "I have a dream" statement, then possibilities and actions will come to us naturally. And the possibilities are endless. In the following pages you will hear about people who "had a dream." They all dove in and worked hard to turn those dreams and possibilities into reality. They saw the potential, and they also saw the challenges within that possibility—the work needed to make it actually happen.

Phase three tends to happen throughout the social change process. Many of us have been part of small groups of thoughtful concerned citizens implementing possibilities, and we have come across the equivalent of experiencing unexpected delays in the repair of that fixer upper. It could be a difference of opinion between those in the group—two or three different ways of doing something, two or three different possibilities. Let's say we want to make the best use of an available community space and have considered using it for a homeless shelter or a local bus depot, but perhaps others want to use it for a child care space. This is where the concept of endless possibilities can be an interesting challenge. Making a decision requires reflection on the initial dreams and curiosity about the other possibilities that are being presented.

This is the point at which we need to meet the challenge of endless possibilities with compassion for each other and each other's ideas. We need to look at what the possibilities are for meeting each of the dreams and the values inherent in those varying dreams. We may not come to agreement immediately; we may never come to agreement; or we could come to agreement several months or years down the line. If and when we do come to agreement, it is like the different spokes on a wheel all working together—a shift from a disparate group of purposes to a wheel in motion.

If we can't come to agreement we need to look at other ways to achieve the dream. For example, we may have a dream of reducing greenhouse gas (GHG) emissions through reducing single-passenger car use. So we decide to create a public bus service. But there is strong resistance to the idea. We could consider putting in car stops for ridesharing instead and, if opinions do change in the future, we can use those as combination bus/car stops.

This same pattern repeats itself in communities, in regions, in provinces and states, in countries, and across countries. Intents differ and conflicts occur if those involved can't find a way to satisfy all those concerned. On an individual basis, it could be two differing opinions about what type of fence to build between neighbors. On a community basis, it could be whether or not to allow secondary suites. On a regional basis, it could be the protection of watersheds versus a company's right to dump its debris in the path of that watershed.

On a global basis, there are people whose intent is profit at all costs, while others' intent is to stop actions creating climate change before those changes destroy the world's inhabitants. We have all been witness to the clash of these two countervailing intents.

Resistance to change

Understanding that resistance to change is a natural human reaction helps us as we walk the labyrinth of social change. Picture a cartoon in which an activist is standing in front of a large crowd. She yells, "Are we against government corruption?" The crowd roars back, "YES!!!" She then asks, "Are we against oil sands and pipelines?" The crowd roars back, "YES!!!" Finally, she shouts, "Are we for Change?" The crowd roars back, "NO!!!" We can laugh with the cartoonist, and we can also learn some realities about social change from it.

First, we tend to be resistant to change. After all, we don't know what real change will bring to our lives, and we have likely become fairly comfortable in the status quo. What will we have to give up if there is real change? And really, it isn't us that should change—it's government and corporations!

So, we want government to change and to make changes. It's so much easier to point the finger at them than it is for us to make changes happen ourselves! After all, the changes we want to see are big—surely they are too big for us to make much of a difference.

Unfortunately, governments rarely make changes unless the politicians know that a substantial portion of the population wants that change. Industry may view a proposed change, such as improving working conditions in vineyards or regulating against harmful pesticides, as compromising their intent to make a profit. And if an industry or corporation is against the change, then government will be even more unwilling, due to potential negative media generated from that industry and the potential loss of campaign funds.

We might also find ourselves wondering what we can actually do in the face of the global and cultural shifts required. Our realm of influence, whether individually or collectively as small groups, isn't that far reaching.

What we can do is engage in possibilities for change in those areas we can influence. Rather than resist change, or fear change, or be angry at government for not making changes, we can have fun and look for possibilities that we can be part of implementing.

The fourth phase in social change is the linking of various actions into the living net. This step includes the effect of threads shifting and changing other threads, creating a multitude of shifts. An accumulation of local actions can produce corresponding changes to regulations with support from government. Let's look at some examples that have happened in the not-too-distant past:

+ Increased accessibility of buildings for people with disabilities
+ The local food movement and increased availability of local food in our stores and restaurants
+ Legal rights available to gay and lesbian couples
+ Changes to the rights of black Americans that were "dreamt of" in Martin Luther King Jr.'s speech.

Instead of being discouraged about the global networks linking capitalist enterprises, we need to remember that we are part of other networks across the globe that connect people and institutions sharing information, knowledge, and lessons learned— all aimed at social justice and harmony with the environment. These influences create a convergence of transformative spaces— not hierarchical but rather an accumulation of localisms. Paul Hawkins, in his book *Blessed Unrest*, described this alternative network as the largest movement the world has ever seen.

Globalization and local spaces

But what about globalization? What about the multinational corporations that have lobbied for laws that give them power over media and government, over the control of information flows? When we speak of globalization we talk about it as an all-encompassing oppression. Global capitalism or other forms of globalization are treated as if they came from elsewhere, not from local spaces. Let's rethink *global*, see where and how it is located in our daily interactions and acknowledge how local interactions in other parts of the world construct our purchases of everything from Italian olive oil to shoes made in China. In *For Space*, Doreen Massey describes how every decision related to a global or trans-continental exchange is carried out in a local place and urges a political understanding that addresses what she calls "the local production of the neoliberal capitalist global."

We can trace what we call global capitalism to local spaces around the world. Let's trace the story of a bottle of wine from Chile. We start with a vineyard in Chile, with the social relations occurring between the people picking the grapes, the owner of the vineyard, and the people turning the grapes into wine. All are local. However, these local spaces are constructing the global—the wine is bottled, carefully packed, and shipped internationally. Through processes of ordering and financing, also carried out from local places, the bottle arrives at an Italian restaurant in the suburbs of Vancouver—and a family celebrating the birthday of their 90-year-old father/grandfather share a glass of wine together. All of these places contain social relations—personal interactions in which corporate globalization is localized.

Imagine a change in one of the local spaces. Pesticides are no longer used on the grapes in Chile for this particular vineyard, and the grapes are certified organic. The workers no longer have to deal with a harmful impact on their health. Soil that was degraded by pesticides will now rejuvenate. The family in Vancouver has the choice of drinking wine from organic grapes. All of these impacts are due to one change in one of the local spaces involved in this global transaction.

What can we learn from this? Rather than glorifying the local and demonizing the global, what we need to ask is what is happening in a local space and does it flow from a corporate agenda or a compassionate agenda. Often it is a combination of both.

The farmers market is a prime example—regulations created by government and corporate entities exist side by side with local produce being served at a farmers market. When we begin to understand that the global is created in the local, we can see that there is, in that space, an opportunity to change the way in which the global is configured. We are not dismissing the extent to which multinationals move their operations when environmental regulations or workers' rights become more stringent than in another country. We are saying that what takes place in each of the local places is what is important.

The world of the multinational corporation is itself created by an accumulation of localisms. It is possible to increase the percent of life-sustaining ways of being that enter into those localisms—think of the organic vineyard. We can also create our own accumulation of life-sustaining localisms. Egg potlucks and sandwiches made from local farm fresh eggs at farmers markets are just the start.

What are the shifts in those alternative localisms?

Together with those we interact with in our homes and local communities and beyond, we create our world through this process of changing and being changed. We hear the objections: What about the influence of corporations? What about systemic inequality built into the system? What about capitalism? We do not argue that these large forces are unimportant; they are important. Our argument is that resistance to such planet-damaging forces is not something that can be done only as resistance. It is not enough to protest; we need to build a life-supporting social order. As we build that new way of being, we will collectively influence the social structures we inhabit. The process is one of iteration, not revolution, even though the changes we seek are revolutionary. Working together, as those whose stories we share here are working together, we will build the basis for a new, life-supporting system to replace the old.

This interrelationship between "the changer and the changed" and the ongoing pattern of changes it reflects is not a new idea, and neither is the idea that this is how positive change in the direction of a life-sustaining world will occur. Joanna Macy and others have written about what they call "the Great Turning"—a shift away from actions that contribute to climate change and towards those that can reduce it.

Macy writes about three dimensions of change that this great turning requires: actions to prevent further damage to the Earth and all its beings; analysis of structural causes behind the damage and the creation of alternatives; and, finally, a shift in consciousness, bringing with it new values to support alternatives. We see the possibilities (and indeed the inevitability) for learning and individual transformation in all three.

In the following chapters, we hear from storytellers how the iterative nature of change, the living net, and the phases of change play out in local communities and influence the broader culture. We start each chapter with an overview of the issue and then intersperse the stories with our reflections. We begin to understand how local is a component of global and we witness evidence of Macy's three dimensions of change and the transformation and learning embedded in that change.

On to the stories!

Stories and Reflections

Sowing the Seeds of Change

Food is a basic necessity of life, and on the surface that would seem to make it very simple. We need food to continue living; we eat. Between these two points, though, lies immense complexity: a global food system that provides abundant food for some and insufficient for others, a huge shipping industry, a thousand human traditions and at least as many opinions. In the Thinking about Food Systems section that follows we will provide a brief summary of the current food system on the Gulf Islands, Vancouver Island, and globally. In Changemakers' Food Stories we hear from our storytellers. We hear about personal choices and relationships with food, creative food organizations, and community food initiatives. Finally we'll take a reflective moment, thinking about how learning illuminates our understanding of food and the food system.

Thinking about Food Systems

The Gulf Islands once supported their inhabitants with foods from the land and sea. Not anymore. It has been estimated that 85 percent of the food eaten on Vancouver Island now comes from off the island and on the Gulf Islands this might be as high as 95 percent. Emergency planners say that Vancouver Island, as a

whole, has only a three- to four-day supply of food should something happen to disrupt food shipments. Beginning with these
statements makes the food system sound rather precarious. For
many people, though, the advantage of the system (including
all the ways foods are gathered, grown, processed, distributed,
consumed, and eventually disposed of) is that it gives us access
to a variety of inexpensive foods grown and produced by others
around the world.

There is a lot of complexity, and many issues, behind this
seemingly simple arrangement. Most of those "others" are working for large businesses practicing mono-crop agriculture. They
use a lot of chemical fertilizers and frequently apply chemical
herbicides and pesticides. Their crops sometimes include geneti-
cally modified organisms. This kind of farming is intensive; labor
is generally poorly paid; and the impact on the environment is
extensive. There are significant emissions of greenhouses gases,
from both fossil fuels and nitrogen-based fertilizers. The use of
agrochemicals (the pesticides, herbicides, and even the fertilizer
itself) pollutes land and water. Run-off doesn't stop at the borders
of the land being farmed this way; it travels into aquifers, into
streams and rivers, and eventually to the oceans. Along the way,
chemical fertilizers can cause extraordinary blooms of algae,
sucking up the oxygen in the water and threatening other species.
On the land and in the ocean, bio-diversity is lost. Not only is each
crop itself a single species and variety, intensive agricultural practices eliminate other plants, insects, animals, and birds from the
location of farming and far beyond.

Is it worth it? Will the industrial agriculture system protect
our food supplies from climate change and ensure that everyone
has enough food? We would love to be optimistic, but it seems
unlikely. Climate change is having a huge impact on the global
food system, just as the global food system contributes to climate
change.

The Intergovernmental Panel on Climate Change (IPCC) estimates that about 20 percent of carbon dioxide emissions in the

United States come from agricultural land use. Almost 15 percent of greenhouse gas emissions come from the farming of livestock. That percentage increases even more when we add to the emissions caused by production the emissions that occur when food is transported throughout North America.

Climate-related damage to crops results from floods, storms, and drought. When food supplies are reduced, prices increase. The 2008 food price crisis, caused, in part, by droughts in grain-exporting nations, foreshadows future impacts on the cost of food. The increase in CO_2 in the atmosphere itself isn't bad for plants; after all, we rely on plants to absorb CO_2 and produce oxygen. Increased atmospheric CO_2 can even lead to increased yields if agricultural practices can be adapted to allow for greater growth, but the changes in practice require increased irrigation. Droughts make this difficult.

Rising oil prices mean higher costs for transporting food, a cost already incorporated into the price of imported food. As we write, oil prices are at historic low levels; the volatility of the energy industry over many years suggests this will not last.

And, while economists tout the advantage of a system that produces inexpensive food, over one billion people in the world are going hungry. In Canada, access to food is also an issue. In March 2016, 863,492 people were assisted by food banks in Canada. This is a 28 percent increase over 2008.

What can we do about all this? There is a growing movement, not just in the Gulf Islands but throughout North America, to increase local organic food production and consumption. Examples on the Gulf Islands include backyard gardens, community gardens, farmers markets, small to medium-sized organic farms, distribution systems for local products, learning forums, and increased storage and processing capacity. This approach to food growing is consistent with the recommendations in the 2013 UN report titled "Wake up before it is too late: Make agriculture truly sustainable now for food security in a changing climate," which emphasizes the need to change how we grow food.

From 2008 to 2013 the number of people using the community gardens on Mayne Island jumped from seven to thirty-three. The results of a survey carried out in 2010 indicate strong support for local produce, whether buying or growing, on Gabriola Island. Over 77 percent of respondents choose local food when available, and over 56 percent grow their own food in the summer.

There is information available for those wanting to become more food self-sufficient. Dan Jason, the owner of Salt Spring Seeds, presents at gardening groups throughout the islands. He demonstrates threshing, describes seed saving strategies, and links climate change, peak oil, and the need to increase food security and food sovereignty on the Gulf Islands. All of his seeds are open-pollinated and non-GMO, ensuring that the seeds are safe to reproduce next year's crops. He also provides free samples of grain seeds at his presentations. His aim is to support the re-establishment of Gulf Island self-sufficiency in grains. As a result of his generosity, several of us are now growing amaranth, while others are growing flax, barley, Ethiopian wheat, buckwheat, and rye. Alan Ostry's 2011 analysis of food self-sufficiency in the Vancouver Island Region indicates why Dan is focusing on increased local production of grains. While the island is 53 percent self-sufficient in eggs and 40 percent self-sufficient in dairy, we are only 1 percent self-sufficient in grain. We are 17.3 percent self-sufficient in vegetables and 16 percent self-sufficient in meat and poultry but only 8.8 percent self-sufficient in fruit.

Farmers markets and farm gate sales, as in other Canadian communities, make it possible for islanders to buy local produce and other local products. While farmers markets and fall fairs have existed on the islands for over sixty years, they played a declining role in supplying produce to consumers when grocery stores began to stock inexpensive year-round produce. Now a renewed interest in local produce has resulted in a number of new vendors and consumers.

Food is a particularly powerful location for learning. The choices we make around food are different from those we make about transportation, shelter, or energy use. Although our choices about food are different in scale from those we make about our home's infrastructure, for example, that's not the only difference. Choices around food are relentless. We make food choices several times every single day, and the range of choices available to many of us is vast. Will we choose to eat something we've prepared ourselves or something someone else has prepared? If we are eating something prepared by someone else, will that someone be working in a locally owned restaurant or an international fast food chain? Or will we purchase something ready-made at the grocery store and, if so, will we have any idea where it was made?

The choices are no less overwhelming at home. Something cooked from scratch? Something from a package? A salad of garden vegetables? What about a simple piece of fruit...is it an apple from our own tree or an apple from New Zealand?

And there are many broader questions about food, too. If we have so many choices, why must some of our neighbors need to rely on the food bank? If our grocery store is full, why are some urban areas "food deserts," where virtually no unprocessed foods are available? And how secure are our choices, really?

Once we begin thinking about food, it's hard to stop!

Changemakers' Food Stories

Personal stories

Leah

Leah, a storyteller involved in local food and cultural initiatives, described the experience of rethinking everything:

> My thinking has changed, and eventually things that were accepted before, taken for granted...aren't anymore, and I feel like I wake up to the importance of every little choice I make. Actually moment to moment to moment is about what is out there—it's not just about me making my choice.

What does Leah mean when she says "what is out there"? She is talking about the interconnectedness between changed modes of thinking and being on the one hand, and on the other our relation to the world around us—to other people, other species, the natural world, and the complex systems that currently construct our society. Leah illustrates the concept of conscious decision-making when describing how a shift to a different mode of thinking changed her day-to-day actions:

> It brings it to what does it actually mean to be present, I mean hyper, super-duper present, in the so-called mundane, in the most mundane day-to-day to day stuff. Am I going to buy this or am I going to buy that? My habit is to buy this…and I have a whole laundry list of reasons why that feels like the right thing to do, and yet, that's the change…it's a whole shift into a different belief about how our moment to moment decisions affect everything.

Free Will

She described how she is now reassessing whether to buy honey that is inexpensive or honey that is local, recognizing that the decision to buy local has a positive impact on the environment, on the local economy, and on people that she has come to know and care about.

At the same time she is very conscious of the deeply held laundry list of reasons that created her habit of buying inexpensive honey from the big box store, not least of which is the financial cost. Her description of how challenging it is to change habits based on the new mode of thinking highlights how elements of our previous stories may still be present as we attempt to shift our actions. Getting deals in order to save money, ease of a plastic bag over remembering the cloth bag, eating oranges flown from Florida and China because we need to treat ourselves or we need oranges in our diet are all part of the collection of rationales that prevent us from acting in the new mode of thinking and being that we have learned.

upon reflection   Leah is exercising her free will—she recognizes that her actions are her choice, not a rule from somewhere else or a story she was told. Different stories are challenging each other as she rethinks her everyday actions.

Rebecca

Rebecca is thirty-two years old. She grew up on one of the Gulf Islands, completed her degree at a university in Eastern Canada, and then moved back to the island with her partner, Alex. Rebecca's conscious decision-making, based on ecological values, is evident in her food choices. To Rebecca, good local food is a value and pleasure. When asked what picture would best demonstrate her everyday life and her values Rebecca described a great big salad of food fresh from her garden.

Integrity

Rebecca has a garden in the local community gardens and another on her own property. She took a permaculture course in order to learn more about self-contained agricultural systems, modeled after natural eco-systems, and she works for pay in islanders' gardens (which she combines with other part-time work). Rebecca is conscious of the impact on the Earth of her various food choices and, whenever possible, chooses the lowest impact while maintaining the pleasure of good food.

Robb

Robb describes food as "one of life's delights—I eat great food—no shortage of variety and flavors...I am very passionate about local food." He wildcrafts (gathers plants, herbs, and fungi from the natural environment) and works in friends' gardens in return for food from those gardens. He believes that local food, grown in a way that incorporates community and stewardship of the environment, plus opportunities to purchase local products, shifts the culture of food from a global food market, with corresponding world-wide transportation, to a local relationship-based culture.

upon reflection   Leah, Rebecca, and Robb all make very deliberate decisions about food—decisions that might be quite different from those of their neighbors. Through gardening, wildcrafting, and focusing on the local, they've shifted their ideas about what is important, and their stories point to some really big ideas. There's the idea that local food contributes to the local economy. There's the idea that local food lessens their own potentially negative impact on the Earth. There's the idea of local food as central to a local, relationship-based culture. It's a lot to see in a jar of local honey!

Shifting the culture of food from a global food market to purchasing local food products promotes a local, relationship-based culture. A local culture can more easily incorporate community and stewardship of the environment.

This is another way in which food is a particularly powerful place for reflection. Thinking of one aspect of food—perhaps changing an imported fruit for one grown locally—can be the first step in a long conversation that leads all the way to a different reordering of the world. Somehow our connections with others are especially clear with food, since there are clearly so many others involved, from grower to seller to cook. We began this book with food because, for so many people, thinking about food is an early step on a much larger journey.

Organization stories
Sharing the land and the vegetables

Two islanders have turned their appreciation for the value of local organic food into a business. Henny and Tom have created Cable Bay Farm on Galiano Island, aimed at providing affordable organic food for Galiano residents (as well as off-island residents) in an environmentally, socially, and financially responsible manner. They have involved the local food program group. Low-income Galiano families have plots in the community section of the farm, and Tom and Henny also donate produce to the food program in return for volunteers who help plant, water, and weed a portion of the farm.

Tom and Henny's approach reminds us of the concept of eco-logical decision-making. They have not only incorporated con-sideration of the environment into their enterprise by growing organically, they have included other community members, ac-knowledging that their farm is only one element in a larger com-munity. Cable Bay Farm is now a cooperative, synergistic part of the island, not just another traditional business with clearly dif-ferentiated vendors and customers.

upon reflection Here is farming in the spirit of compassion. Cable Bay Farm is a place of compassion towards the land, and also towards the community—those who need to share in the food that is grown but who perhaps lack the means to partici-pate as "consumers" and those who want to work on an organic farm but perhaps lack the skills to create one.

Artists and soap-sellers

Another example of food enterprise on the islands is Lulu's Local. Although no longer in business, it was influential and remains a good example of an innovative approach to increasing access to local food. (The niche it filled is now served by the local grocery store.) The board members of Lulu, a performing arts group, were discouraged by their reliance on erratic government funding for the arts. Leah describes what happened next:

> *The roots of Lulu's Local started a few years ago when we part-nered with Longwood Brew Pub and created Lulu's lager.... It felt like a way to hold a space for art in the community in a different kind of way. Even someone who doesn't go to a concert might buy a product and participate.*
>
> *And then it moved into collaborating with Margot—she made soap. The whole thing was fun, and interesting and lively...and we talked about connections and we talked about community*

and we talked about how we weren't just selling products. At the same time there was a whole world that was swirling around it that felt really good—enjoyable.

That moved to talking with Wayne at Village Foods [the manager at a local grocery store] and asking whether, if we were to collaborate with a bunch of artisan producers from the community and beyond, would they be interested in letting us set up a stand in the store, and he said that he thought there was a niche that could be filled...a need for a distributorship in the region that would focus on local producers and local vendors. There are a couple of people that are doing that but they're distributing to a much larger region. So, we basically explored the idea for a couple of years...looked at feasibility and then just decided to jump in and see if it actually was feasible.... So that's when we launched the pilot.

Any profit from Lulu's Local went to funding the arts on the islands. In the meantime a range of local artisan products became available in grocery stores year round, providing island residents with access to locally produced artisan food and bath products.

Lulu's Local operated from a different mode of thinking as well. According to Leah, connections were a core component of this social enterprise: "Just going around and seeing how people live who are working in the community and with the land.... It's not just the beauty in seeing how people are connected to place. It is the conversations that come up around it and the connectedness that comes up that I appreciate. I get to go to the tea farm. We're on hugging terms. That's really cool!"

From Leah's perspective this approach flipped the traditional way of doing business on its head. Instead of profit being the overarching goal, "the larger umbrella, or the larger container, is around culture—the support for our cultural economy, both artisan culture and food economy. We were trying to hold it in that space."

Out of this work she has come to realize the challenge of producing and buying local within the current regulatory system. "The whole labeling process itself is challenging for small, local food producers. I wonder if it is deliberately made cumbersome and expensive." Processes that make sense for multi-national companies, or even large non-organic farms, don't make sense for the small, local artisan or farmer.

upon reflection As people contemplate their relationships with food and with their local community, and also their need to sustain themselves, it is a logical step to consider a food-based business. In doing so it becomes apparent that the processes set up for the convenience of large corporations don't work very well for small, local businesses. Exploring the reasons for the challenging processes, or even just looking for ways to avoid the most cumbersome regulations, can be a way for those exploring business ideas, and their customers, to learn more about the way our society is structured, and for whose benefit.

Community stories
The 100 mile diet

Vicki tells the story of community gardens that weren't functioning well when she arrived on Mayne Island:

I like to garden, and the circumstances of where I was at when I came over to the island didn't allow me to do that. There was a space over at the community center, but it was very poorly set up. The infrastructure was there, but there wasn't any gardening happening because it had been left to be developed on an individual basis. You bought the wood and you brought in the soil, and then it was your little plot and you were responsible for your individual container. I think it had been going for a few years, and there were only seven people who had plots. Most of the ground was unused, and there were blackberry brambles all over the place, but someone loaned me one of the existing plots.

It was evident that someone had made an attempt to set up community gardens prior to Vicki's arrival on the island. But why did the attempt not live up to the possibilities? Vicki proposed the following reason:

> I was looking and thought, "Gee, there's so much potential here, but this needs a group of people; it's just not going to happen otherwise." It's daunting for people to do everything required to maintain their own small garden. It needs a whole different way of managing it. People need to see themselves as contributing to the whole, not just to their plot.

She then worked with others to restructure the management of the gardens and raised funds to make it work as a shared effort. The number of people using the garden jumped from seven to thirty-three.

Louis, another Mayne Island resident, believed that other reasons also contributed to the community garden finally working.

"So what made the time right for the gardens—what had an influence? That was just when the 100-mile diet came along, then that whole concept of food security and growing your own food. Before that nobody was doing as much gardening." What Louis touches on is the extent to which influences from off the islands contribute to the dialogue on the islands. *The 100 Mile Diet* is a book written by a Vancouver couple, Alisa Smith and J. B. McKinnon, about their experience of eating only food grown within 100 miles of where they were living. National radio programs hosted discussions about *The 100 Mile Diet*, and the book was on the best seller list in Canada. In 2009 a television show called *The Hundred Mile Challenge* featured six couples attempting a diet consisting of food grown within 100 miles of their homes. People across the continent, including the Gulf Islands, became part of the discussion about global food systems and the value of eating locally grown food—the living net in action.

Living Net

Brian, a fellow islander who had been involved in creating local-food community dinners around the same time *The 100 Mile Diet* was published, suggested that there are ways in which members of the community "can create the 'time is right' by advocates trying to get a critical mass going." From his perspective it was the synergy of a range of factors, including the community dinners and the restructuring of the community gardens, lining up with *The 100 Mile Diet*, that created the increase in local food growing.

upon reflection   Where's the learning in this? No doubt there was lots of learning—how to garden, how to get along in a group, and all of that—but this local learning finds an echo and an amplification in the writing of Smith and McKinnon. In their everyday life, they looked at a "truth"—Canada relies on imported food—and questioned it. Their challenge to the usual story of the supermarket encourages us to look at other societal stories and ask "But what if that is not true?"

Potatoes in the rain

The *Gabriola Commons* is a 26-acre piece of land near Gabriola Island's village core. It is owned, cared for, and stewarded by the community and is accessible to all island residents. The Commons constitution lists its three important purposes: "To hold, protect, and steward the property on Gabriola Island known as the 'Gabriola Commons' as a public amenity, with green spaces, hiking trails, and public exhibition, performance, and meeting spaces for the use and enjoyment of the public in perpetuity; to preserve the ecological qualities of the Gabriola Commons; and to promote and demonstrate sustainable agricultural practices." The property holds a multi-purpose community building, approximately 100 community garden plots, a Yurt that provides space for creative workshops and activities, a community kitchen, a Sustainability Centre, a home for the community bus, and a range of community programs.

Judith, one of the Common's founders, describes a potato-harvesting work bee in the rain on the Gabriola Commons:

That's what makes the heart just sing, working with people and half of them you don't know, you've never worked together before—and everybody feels just so damn good. We had one Saturday harvesting the potatoes because Brian Minter [a local gardening expert] had said this is going to be a really difficult winter—you've got to get those potatoes out of the ground or.... So we called for the work bee, and it was raining and it was miserable. And a lot of people came to that one, 10 or 12 people out in the kitchen garden taking potatoes, and it was yucky, but it was fabulous, and you just could almost have heard the singing and the music coming from this. It was great.

upon reflection   What does this story have to do with learning and change? Surely there isn't much to be learned from a group of soggy islanders, gathering potatoes that they could presumably just as well buy at the supermarket. But the collective action in this case was at least as important as the potatoes—more important, if you ask Judith. The people at the work bee—the singing, digging, muddy group—were modeling, for themselves and for each other and for anyone else they talked to about this special day, a way of collectively being together that had nothing to do with consumerism and everything to do with shared delight in the harvest. Shining practice in the garden, everyone covered with mud and grinning from ear to ear!

A final reflection on food

We began with food because it is something that we choose daily, something that everyone chooses, and therefore something that is always available for us to question and to learn from. We might find the learning in a sudden revelation: Anna's egg reveals that food safety is perhaps not as straightforward as we thought. The learning might come from seeing an example: harvesting potatoes in the mud can be a joyful opportunity for building community, not just an encounter with, well, mud! The learning might come through compassion: the farmer not only grows food for the farmer and food buyers but also for others, and in a way that shows kindness to the Earth. Revelation, example, and compassion—all are present in the food we eat or don't eat.

When we look up from the specific stories and think about our broader experience of food, we find even more to think about. For many people, learning about food means learning about family traditions. "My Mom did it this way, so I do too," we imagine saying. But really, how many of us live that way now? We may instead be drawn to the traditions of our neighbors and friends rather than our own. (Mary is personally lukewarm on the idea of salt cod, a favorite of her mother's, but drawn to her childhood Ukrainian neighbors' egg noodles.) We may be more motivated by our concern for climate change and see every choice of an imported food as an opportunity to wield that sword. We may be motivated by our compassion to follow a vegan or vegetarian path.

We find, too, that there are gaps in our knowledge of food, and differences in the way we learn about it. We may swap gardening tips with a neighbor half our age instead of seeking wisdom within our own families—for many of us, the previous generation didn't garden. We may be inspired by the many events in our lives to wonder with compassion…to find ways to explore ideas around food that are not attacks on what we have known or on the cherished traditions of others but rather attempts to explore and ask "what if" questions that may give rise to all kinds of learning.

To ponder

Reflect on your community. What percentage of the food consumed is grown outside your community, your region, or your country? What actions have people and businesses taken to increase access to local organic food in your community? In your community has there been an increase in backyard gardens, community gardens, farmers markets, organic farms, distribution systems for local products, learning forums, and storage and processing capacity? How is the learning and knowledge being transferred within your community as well as between your community and others across the continent and beyond? Have government agencies responded to the culture shift in communities with any policy changes or initiatives? How have your personal food habits shifted as you learned different stories about food through compassion, wisdom, and practice?

Walls and Roofs

Different stories

 Thinking about Shelter

Like food, shelter is a necessity of life. It protects us from the elements and provides space for eating, sleeping, and all the activities of daily living. The Coast Salish people built homes just over 3,000 square feet in size, which housed several families. They used local cedar for these communal spaces, with no private ownership of the building or land. There was a relationship with the Earth embedded in their approach—the Coast Salish perceiving their role as stewards and their relationship as interconnected with the land rather than dominating it. Early settlers on the Gulf Islands used wood cut from their homesteads to build their homes, and families lived in homes under 1,000 square feet. They did believe in property ownership and mostly lived with their immediate families. Resource extraction and farming were the primary occupations.

In our current culture, large houses are often perceived as a sign of success. In 1975 the average size of a Canadian house was 1,050 square feet, while in 2010 new homes being built were an average of 1,950 square feet. At the same time, the number of people living in a house dropped from 3.5 down to 2.5. The average size of a new single-family house in the United States was

2,438 square feet in 2009. A larger home means more of every-thing: more space, certainly, but also more fuel to heat it, more furniture to fill it, and more building supplies to build it. It also means more waste in the landfill. In urban areas, older homes are often torn down to make way for the new. In Vancouver, for example, nearly a thousand older homes have been demolished each year since 2012 to make way for the new.

One advantage of the new houses compared to those of the early settlers and even to those of the 1970s is that they are built to much higher energy efficiency standards. The 1,000-square-foot house of 100 years ago may have required the same amount of heat as today's much larger 2,000-square-foot house.

If we think back to the time when Coast Salish people were building their large multi-family homes, and even to the days when the settlers built their smaller private homes, building materials were either entirely or largely local. Not anymore. Decisions about sourcing building and finishing materials are usually based on price and quality, on economic thinking rather than whether they are locally or sustainably produced—ecologi-cal thinking. Building sites reflect this. In western Canada, for instance, cedar siding typically is made in Canada, but the nails we hammer it on with are made in China, and the hammer or air-nailer likely is too.

Throughout the world, many people cannot afford to buy a house due to high prices that have resulted from real estate spec-ulation. (International surveys consistently include Vancouver among the ten least affordable cities worldwide.) The challenges of affordable housing are complex and find their root in our eco-nomic system and the speculative nature of the real estate mar-ket. In Canada, the federal, provincial, and local governments have all, at various points over the past 50 years, initiated pro-grams, studies, and policies to respond to the issue.

There is a growing number of people throughout North America choosing to create their shelter in a different way than the individual and expensive norm described above. The homes Rebecca and Briony built, and the homes the Mudgirls build, described later in this chapter, are examples drawn from the Gulf Islands. We hear other stories too, stories of groups of people collectively reshaping shelter options, building materials, and structure as well as the composition of those sharing the space and property ownership.

Changemakers' Shelter Stories

Rebecca

Rebecca and her partner's house is just over 800 square feet, much smaller than most new homes. They chose to build a home of this size because a smaller building footprint leaves more of the natural earth intact and uses less materials and less energy. Every part of the house is thoughtfully designed, from the size to the materials. Rebecca and her partner used stick framing, as do most homes in western Canada, but the infill is made from waste wood chips, gathered on the island, together with clay from their property. Their choice of materials includes an electric on-demand water heater, primarily recycled windows with a couple of new windows from a community selling site, pillars instead of a full foundation to reduce the use of concrete (one twentieth of what it would have been if a full foundation had been poured), and rain water collection. They have plans for solar hot water heating. There was minimal waste created in the construction process—only two bags of garbage at the end of the framing and roofing process.

 upon reflection The various practices that Rebecca and her partner are following to reduce their impact on the Earth can be examples for all of us—the kind of thoughtful action that really is shining practice. One of the things about the process they chose is the way the house-building itself contributed to building the community they are part of. Several friends gathered

to help prepare and install the infill for the walls, and the progress of the house was a topic of conversation for a much wider
circle. A transformative space was created and became part of
the living net.

There is another way the choices they are making can have an impact, too, giving rise to moments of sudden realization—a quiet
wielding of the sword of wisdom. At 800 square feet, the house
seems small compared to the average new home built in Canada.
And it is small—according to 2009 statistics, the average new
home in Canada is more than twice as big. The same statistics
say the average new home in Great Britain is just over 800 square
feet; in urban centers in China, the average is just under 650. The
Canadian 1,948 square feet isn't just an inevitable result of cold
weather; in Sweden the average new home is just 893 square
feet. Exploring Rebecca's house, and thinking about her ideas
and choices, encourages us to challenge our own ideas of what is
enough and what is really necessary. Checking international statistics might encourage us to think about our usual choices even
more critically.

Of course, it is Rebecca's intention to live a satisfying life, not
primarily to challenge others to reflect on their housing choices.
Rebecca has every intention of inhabiting her house fully, with
her partner, her dog, and her many interests. Hers is not a life of
deprivation to prove a point, but a life lived well and fully. The
idea of shining practice is embodied in this kind of life—a life
worth living is also one that inspires and perhaps challenges,
and is also deeply satisfying for the person living it. Who would
spend their precious human life doomed to be nothing more than
a good example?

Briony

Briony, another islander, describes her home on Salt Spring Island
as a "100-mile home." Local salvaged fir and cedar were milled for
her home. Slate shingles and a clawfoot bathtub were obtained

from local demolitions and renovations. She refused to use any materials containing chemicals harmful to the environment or humans, and despite this challenge she still managed to comply with building code regulations. For instance, she had hoped to use sheep wool insulation, but the building code required the wool to be sprayed with a fire retardant, so instead she used some pre-owned Rockwool insulation (consistent with the building code) from a local supplier of recycled construction materials.

upon reflection Compassion is not just emotion but action. Briony avoided using harmful chemicals in her home, thus protecting her own health and but also the health of others who worked on the home and others in the environment where the building materials are produced. Reflecting on potential dangers and acting to avoid them reaches out, spreading compassion to the whole world; the practice of environmental protection while building a home expresses that sense of compassion through thoughtful reflection, purposeful choice, and hours of action. As she built her home she reached out to her network of friends, builders, and suppliers. Each of them, through witnessing a home built with integrity, could see the initial dream, then possibilities being put into action. The influence of this building spread beyond Briony's property.

The Mudgirls Natural Building Collective

The Mudgirls Natural Building Collective, a group of women living throughout coastal British Columbia, use mostly unprocessed natural and recycled materials to construct natural buildings. They build homes for clients, host workshops to teach building skills to others, and trade hours between themselves to build their own homes. Many of the structures they build are small and are built under the radar of officialdom. As a result, the Mudgirls can apply the principles of natural building without being tied to regulations designed for traditional forms of construction. They use rocks already on site for the foundation; dirt, clay, straw and woodchips for the walls; driftwood and other salvaged logs for the wood components of the structures; recycled windows; and recycled glass bottles as stained glass windows. The purpose of the collective, described by Rose, is "to use natural and recycled materials and to empower people and ourselves."

There is more significance to the Mudgirls' story than the materials they select for building, though. The structures of the collective and of the work parties acknowledge the historic, systemic, and cultural challenges facing women. Rose describes how the Mudgirls have agreed that they are a woman's collective, not to exclude men but rather to support women's learning:

> It would be hard to deny that a gender dynamic exists in our culture, with women tending to be a bit self-conscious, especially if it is in a male-dominated type of industry. Women tend to defer to men's opinions in areas like that, and so we just want to avoid that possibility altogether.

Their work parties include both men and women. However, having women as the cob home builders supports a culture that counteracts traditional gender behaviors. Rose explains, "Usually it's a lot of young women [in the workshops] who have never done any building before—not exclusively but primarily—and they've expressed that it's a supportive environment." Some of the participants have described the work parties as transformative. "People have told us that they have had quite a profoundly enlightening experience." Many also described feeling empowered, "because they are usually doing a lot of physical labor, maybe stuff they've never done before—it's not just mixing mud with your feet. They may be learning how to cut down trees and use power tools they've never used before, as well as just being part of building a house."

Mindful Practice

upon reflection   The confidence to rely on oneself rather than experts, a way of communicating that emphasizes self-responsibility, and allowing multiple realities rather than an "us against them" or victim response, all stem from a different way of understanding the world and a desire, on the part of the Mudgirls, to take action based on their values rather than a desire for profit. The story of the Mudgirls brings another element into system shifting. When people operate from a different way of thinking and being, from a place of ecological decision-making rather than economic self-interest, ways of governance and management shift as well. The traditional hierarchical approach is not congruent with the new societal story.

Again we witness a local action that spreads out into the world. Workshop participants may come from numerous different countries. Hands-on experience creates opportunities for numerous living net connections to expand a new societal story beyond the site of the workshop. Rose mentioned that she has heard back from many participants who have described stories of transformative changes in their lives.

Policy intersections for natural building

As much as possible the Mudgirls Collective stays outside the regulatory system: "You know—don't ask permission." Rose describes the need for a "try to stay under the radar" approach combined with pure natural building, while at the same time working within the system for natural building regulatory change, with some compromise of natural building principles:

Some people, like Ann and Gord Baird, have taken a completely different approach—they have chosen to work with engineers, and they've actually worked for policy change. They work to educate people, and they've built a cob house to code. Their approach is completely different and they've had a lot of success with it—they've built a beautiful house, and that kind of work is very important because they have worked to change building codes and to make more and more engineers and city workers aware and open minded.

While they provide the option for owners to build outside the regulatory system, the Mudgirls Natural Building Collective also build with permits. The decision is up to the owner of the building and dependent upon the use and size of the building. They have had some interesting interactions with regulations, and officials enforcing the regulations, interactions that highlight the challenge of building in ways the current construction industry does not quite expect.

When a client asked the Mudgirls Natural Building Collective to build a green roof, they experienced the shock of a government/corporate "truth." They discovered that, due to the growing popularity of green roofs, the government had moved to include guidelines for green roofs in the building code. This added a new requirement to the construction process that produced some negative consequences.

We've done quite a few of them [green roofs] using a pond liner on the roof—you use the slope and soil, whatever, to weight it. Then all of a sudden there comes a code for how to do a green roof and now you can't just lay the liner down—you have to use this glue.

Because government regulations aren't created at the local level, they often seem, to those most affected by them, to appear out of thin air. Where did this change come from? From the Mudgirls' perspective, it did not seem to be solving a problem they had noticed with green roofs.

Tracking the origin of the change led to the provincial government's Home Protection Office (HPO). Their 2008 report on green roofs stated that "a number of local governments have been considering mandating this type of roof in new construction of various types." Four out of the five home warranty companies, approved to offer home warranties under the Home Protection Act informed the government, in 2007, that they would not provide warranties for buildings with living roofs. The government appointed a task force, composed of representatives from the warranty industry, condominium owners, the green building industry, installation contractors, developers, architects, and local government to consider how to make green roofs fit under this kind of warranty. There was no one representing individuals building their own homes, and almost certainly no one representing the many independent contractors who often work with single-family home builders.

One of the group's recommendations, and the only one implemented immediately, was "Advise local governments against mandating extensive green roofs in residential construction at this time" (HPO, 2008). The letter to all local governments in British Columbia included the following statement:

> *The task group noted that, while it is technically feasible to design, install, and maintain a green roof properly, the probability that this would be done is considerably less than certain at this time. This is due to factors such as the lack of experience with these systems in British Columbia, the limited supply of skilled labor, the absence of accepted standards and minimum levels of quality control, and the inability to ensure that strata corporations discharge their responsibilities for maintenance properly. Although there are proprietary green roof systems available in British Columbia, the market penetration of these systems is quite limited at present.*
>
> *Consequently, the task group identified a number of risks that would arise from failure to design, install, and maintain green roofs properly. These include the failure of the membrane, leading to water penetration, the destruction of plant material through drought or other influence, economic losses for homeowners if failures are not covered by home warranty insurance, liability claims for local governments and catastrophic failures for home warranty insurance providers if green roof failures were widespread.*

We've quoted this statement at length because it reflects the various interests represented on the Task Force so well. Insurance, legality, installation and maintenance responsibilities—all were reflected. Local governments each responded in their own way to the preceding concerns. Due to the risks identified in the letter, the regional district responsible for building permits for Salt Spring Island implemented a policy requiring a warranty for green roofs. Rose tells the story:

> We were working on a small cabin on Salt Spring, and they wanted a cabin with green roof that was to code—so, in order to make this happen now, you have to buy the glue from the pond liner company, and to lay the liner down you have to use the glue.

The Roofing Contractors Association of British Columbia (RCABC, one of the Task Force members) provides the British Columbia Green Roofs warranty. Their warranty is valid only if the installer carries out the directions provided by the supplier of the liner and glue: "Only waterproofing membrane systems that are fully adhered and have an accepted protection layer installed above qualify for coverage under the RGC Guarantee Program." These guidelines make sense from a risk and warranty perspective. The regional district and the RCABC want to be sure they are not on the hook for problems created by the unknown dangers of green-roof construction. But is it coincidental that the decision also requires the company's products to be purchased?

> So, on a hot summer day a couple of the Mudgirls are trying to lay this pond liner down and the glue is bubbling and rippling and it is impossible to get it smooth. There are horrendous fumes, and first they feel giddy, then they feel headachy, then by the end of the day they're just totally sick from the fumes.... Something that would have taken an hour to lay down and smooth out and put the dirt on top of it, now takes an entire day and they're basically poisoned from it. They had a hangover the next day—it had that kind of lingering affect.

When setting the policy that required the glue, not one of the regulatory bodies appears to have considered this negative side effect of that policy. It also isn't obvious that they spent any time looking at green roofs installed without the glue. From the perspective of the Mudgirls Natural Building Collective, the result was detrimental in terms of both time and health, and didn't appear, to them, to make any difference to the end result. While the Mudgirls carried out the policy for the cabin on Salt Spring it is unlikely that they will accept any future work involving building green roofs to code if the glue requirement is still in place. However benign the intent of the task force's work, the result may well be fewer green roof installations and in some cases, at least, a return to more highly manufactured roofing materials.

Another interesting disconnect between policy and the practicalities of natural building was experienced by a client of the Mudgirls Natural Building Collective. This disconnect, as Rose explains, came directly from the corporate world:

> We had a client on Salt Spring who had built a conventional house insulated with dense foam insulation and hired us to put natural plaster on the inside wall. When he later went to insure the house, the little form [the insurers] have said "What's your wall material?" and they didn't have a place for him to put a check mark for natural plaster. So they were suggesting to him that they weren't able to insure the house...which would mean that he wouldn't be able to keep his mortgage.

The homeowner is now placed in a challenging situation, all because he made a decision, based on environmental values, to use natural plaster for the walls in his conventionally built home. His options include replacing the natural plaster with traditional wall material such as drywall, selling his home, or negotiating with the insurer.

He decided to negotiate through demonstrating the extent to which natural plaster is fire safe relative to drywall, an accepted wall material:

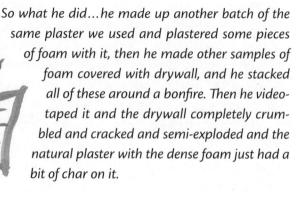

So what he did…he made up another batch of the same plaster we used and plastered some pieces of foam with it, then he made other samples of foam covered with drywall, and he stacked all of these around a bonfire. Then he video-taped it and the drywall completely crumbled and cracked and semi-exploded and the natural plaster with the dense foam just had a bit of char on it.

Transformative
Space

He then took the video to the insurance company, introducing another story into the space, and, as Rose related,

He was able to get an exception—they're not able to do this for everyone, but for that particular house they approved his insurance.

upon
reflection   The story of the green roof and the insurance company's list of wall surfaces gives us a light into the intersection between new and old stories. Just as the regulations regarding the inspection of eggs eventually shifted to contain some of the "new societal story," there are possibilities for eventual changes in both the green roof regulations and the wall choice list. The video of the charred drywall next to the barely singed natural plaster is the start of policy change. As Leonard Cohen says "That's how the light gets in."

Flexibility and simplicity

In 1996, when Robbie and Mary moved into their owner-built home on Gabriola, the building department assured them it was the smallest legal dwelling in the Regional District of Nanaimo. At exactly 400 square feet, the compact house had everything necessary—kitchen, living room, dining area, home office, and even a shower room separate from a half-bath with composting toilet and sink. The secret was flexibility. The shower and half-bath were each in a separate room, but otherwise the house was entirely open. The piano served as a room divider, giving the bedroom a sense of privacy. The home office was tucked into an alcove. At night, the couch and chair folded down and pushed together to become a bed:

> *It was actually quite elegant and baffling for people. They would see a love seat and chair and would say, "Where do you sleep?" The multiple-use thing was really high on my list of priorities.* [Mary]

They had been inspired by their experiences in Asia. "We'd just come back from two years in South Korea," Robbie recalls, "and we had discovered *Your Money or Your Life* there." The message they took from the book was that a smaller home would mean less work, less money, and more importantly, more freedom. It didn't feel like deprivation. "We were pretty happy living in our 200 square-foot apartment in Seoul," Mary remembers. "We had room for everything: doing the laundry, relaxing.... We even had people over for Christmas dinner."

Robbie and Mary have warm memories of friends in Seoul, in particular a family whose four generations (ancient mother, middle-aged couple, their son and his wife, plus a baby) all lived in a neighboring apartment.

> *It was a small two-bedroom apartment by any standards. And the old woman, who was ending her life, took up a whole bedroom—that was not flexible. She was there. But the rest of it....*
> *I remember having a fancy dinner in their bedroom one time, which was possible because they slept on a yo [a Korean sleeping mat] on the floor, which just rolls up and goes away. The bedroom became just a big room with a lovely wardrobe, armoire style. So, there was no reason why you couldn't use it as a dining room. Everyone sits on the floor at the table. It made it extremely flexible, and that was the kind of vibe we were after.*

However, the building code does not share an Asian sensibility when it comes to flexible space.

So, we said, really, how small a house could we be happy with? We initially thought 16' × 20' but we found that that wasn't going to be a legal house. There is a minimum size. There's not a minimum total floor area but there is a minimum size in the building code for each different function in the house and you can't overlap. You must have a dining area of a certain size, a kitchen of a certain size, a bathroom, a bedroom.... When you add them all up the smallest footprint that we could fit it into was 20' × 20'— 400 square feet.

The reaction of friends and family included some negative opinions. Some people seemed really shocked at the size they were talking about.

People thought that we were naïve and wouldn't really be happy in a house that size: "They're kids—they think they can live on crumbs and be happy." We were in our forties.... So we weren't kids!

One of the early influences for both Robbie and Mary was Henry David Thoreau, especially, in this context:

...his very evocative writing about the typical house owner going down the road pulling his house and his barn behind him...the burden of big houses and complex lives as opposed to simplicity. I absolutely feel that. The simpler you can make your life the more freedom you can have. And there's nothing else I want more than that.

Egg of Wisdom

Tiny homes are now becoming more and more common as people across North America realize that they can live comfortably in a small space and don't have to have the burden of a large mortgage attached to their home. While regulations have still not kept up in most jurisdictions, there are websites where people needing a place to park their tiny home can hook up with those wanting people to locate on their land. There are also tiny homes registered as mobile homes so that they can be located wherever mobile homes are legal.

upon reflection Robbie and Mary's story is about living simply, and a tiny flexible home was part of that story. However, their story bumped up against the story and ideal of the big house, both within their own family and with building regulations. Today we are witnessing a shift in that story as more people are realizing the benefits of no mortgage and less house to clean and maintain. And, as is usually the case, government policies are slowly catching up to the new story, as it moves from "You're doing what?" to part of mainstream culture.

Cooperatives on Hornby

Hornby Island cooperatives are not a single organization but rather a reflection of the culture on Hornby Island, a culture that responds to collective community needs by creating buildings and organizations that are built by members of the community and collectively managed. Hilary and HB Brown, who arrived on Hornby Island in the 1930s, initiated the first cooperative and were key players in many of those that followed. Doug, a long-time resident of Hornby Island, provides us with stories of various cooperative ventures, from pathways to community halls.

Hornby Island provides numerous examples of cooperative building. The residents have built a store, school, community hall, recycling center, seniors' center, and seniors' housing, using a cooperative, community-based model. Affordable housing, based on a land trust, donated land, and a cooperative model, is in progress. In this section we will hear about some of those structures and how they came about. In the Cooperative Economics chapter we will come back to the Hornby cooperatives and look at the economic side of the store and school that were cooperatively built by the community.

The attitude of "Let's just build this as a community" is evident in many buildings shared by residents of the island. The community built the Hornby Island Recycling Depot (HIRD) in 1978. At the forefront of the recycling movement, the recycling center became a model for other communities throughout British Columbia and the world. We describe its story in more detail in Chapter 8: There is No Away.

Another cooperatively built structure is the Community Hall. According to Doug, "It's a unique-looking building, really—really hippy looking. We've just added an addition to it sixteen to twenty years later, and it just keeps going on—another cooperative effort by just people." The residents use the hall for community gatherings, music concerts, meetings, and potlucks.

Hornby Island community members have also initiated seniors and affordable housing projects. They used a Community Land Trust model to support the financing, with funds donated from both residents and visitors to the island. "The seniors' housing: It just went ahead. A group of people formed a society—The Hornby Island Elder Housing Society—and they started raising funds. We raised funds for a number of years and finally bought a property. And then we started building a unit, then a second unit, then a third unit. As the rental came in from the earlier units, that helped pay for the fourth, fifth, and sixth units. So that has been a great success." As in co-housing and cooperative housing models elsewhere, the residents work together collectively, with the society, to manage the five-acre property.

upon reflection Hornby Island is a particularly good example of a community that gets thing done without waiting for a lot of outside intervention. This might partly be a response to its location. It's far from isolated, but it is a two-ferry-plus-a-drive trip to get from Hornby to Vancouver Island, and ferry service is limited. It's partly just the culture of the island itself. For many years there were no building inspections or inspectors on Hornby, and the owner-built home was by far the most common kind. People who were looking for a community where they could just buy a home and move in were not likely to choose the island. Hornby was also a new community for many Americans who had left the United States to avoid the draft during the '60s and '70s. Once you've questioned the stories society tells you, so thoroughly that you've questioned your way right out of your country of birth, you're likely more willing than the average person to question the local school division when it tells you there's a two-year wait for a new schoolroom.

"We can do it ourselves" is a great rallying cry. It is the cry of those who see the way that things are usually done and ask "Why?" It opens the arms of compassion, turning many hands to the service of the environment, children, and old people. And it helps create the world of good practice, where individuals work together and model a new way of being in the world.

To ponder

What is the average size of home in your neighborhood, community, region, and country? What materials are used to build housing in your community? Is there much waste, or are there ways the materials going to landfill have been reduced? Are there innovative approaches to housing that include reduced size, flexibility in use of rooms, natural materials, reduced or zero waste, or re-use of old homes? What type of ownership models are in place? Are there examples of cooperative living, cooperative building, and/or joint ownership of common amenities? How have your personal approaches to shelter shifted as you learned different stories about building through compassion, wisdom, and practice?

Moving Forward

Just do it!

Thinking about Transportation

In the western world transportation can be summed up in two words: fossil fuel. We fuel our cars, our planes, our trains, and our boats with different forms of fossil fuel. There are exceptions, such as electricity, hydrogen, and biodiesel, but right now these are the exception rather than the rule.

In 2015 transportation was the second largest source of CO_2e (Carbon Dioxide equivalent) in Canada, at 173 Megatons (Mt) CO_2e, accounting for 24 percent of Canada's Greenhouse gas emissions. The following chart shows the breakdown of transportation uses and corresponding Mt of greenhouse gas emissions.

According to the World Energy Council, Canada's per capita transport emissions were 4.89 Tonnes (T—a metric ton, roughly equivalent to the Imperial ton and to 1.1 US tons) CO_2e in 2014; the United States per capita transport emissions were 5.25 T CO_2e, whereas in Europe the per capita emissions were just 1–2 T CO_2e. Those of us in North America need to question why the difference. And, according to Canadian government projections, emissions are expected to increase in Canada, not decrease.

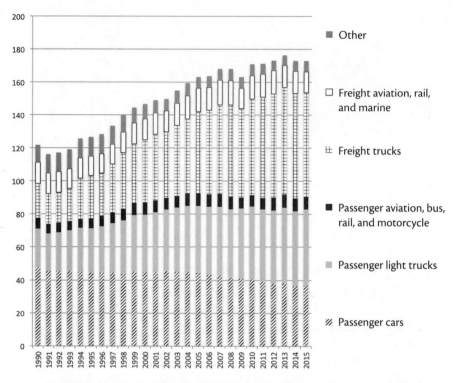

Canada Transportation Emissions (Mt CO2e) 2015. Credit: Environment and Climate Change Canada.

The emission factors involved in passenger transportation include the need or desire for people to move themselves from one location to another, the mode of transportation (bus, truck, bike, etc.), the fuel efficiency of the mode of transportation, the type of fuel used, and the availability of non-emission–producing modes of transport. From 1991 to 2015 the fuel efficiency of vehicles improved. However, during the same period Canadians increased their use of light trucks over more fuel-efficient cars, thus increasing total emissions.

The increased ease of transporting ourselves from one side of the continent to the other in the past 60 years has dramatically impacted our work and settlement patterns. In North America our communities and road systems are based on the use of a car to get from one place to another. Commuting to work, one person per vehicle, has become a key feature of today's working world. We hear about traffic gridlocks on the morning news and the usual government solution is to put in more roads and widen the roads that are already there.

Suburbs and urban sprawl have been created out of the assumption that we all have cars to get us to work, school, and other activities. Cyclists and pedestrians have lobbied for safe bike and walking paths, as roads have become increasingly unsafe for them. While there has been some increase in bike paths and pedestrian crossings, North American roadways are still primarily devoted to automotive vehicles.

The lobbying and marketing power of the large car manufacturers and the oil and gas industry have kept fossil-fuel vehicles as the primary mode of ground transportation for over 100 years. Attempts to create electric vehicles were stymied in the mid to late 1990s, as depicted by the documentary *Who Killed the Electric Car?* According to the documentary, automakers and the oil industry did not want electric cars to become mainstream and eat into their profits. Today electric vehicles are slowly becoming a viable alternative to gas and diesel vehicles. However, they still accounted for only 1 percent of the North American market in 2016.

The greenhouse gas emission factors involved in freight transportation include the distance products are transported, the weight and bulk of the products, the amount of non-local products purchased, the type of fuel used, and the type of transport used. While an antidote might be to buy local products, the majority of products we buy are manufactured outside of North America and Europe due to low labor costs and less stringent environmental regulations in countries such as China and India.

In the following pages we will hear how some people have challenged our society's love affair with owning and driving fossil-fuel vehicles. In subsequent chapters we will look at how cooperative economics and rethinking waste can help reduce freight transportation emissions.

Changemakers' Transportation Stories

Personal transportation

Rebecca's prime modes of transportation are cycling and walking, while Robb uses an electric vehicle and his sailboat in addition to walking. Anna's primary mode of transportation is her electric bike.

Car stops

Barry, a member of a local transportation group, invented the car stops on Pender Island. He describes how he came up with the idea:

> With a population of approximately 2,200 I knew that we would never have a bus. It just wasn't going to happen—economically it doesn't work unless you have a really good ridership. So, I thought rather than bus stops why not have something that looks almost the same and call it car stops?

Car stops provide places for people to wait if they require a lift; they are marked by a Car Stop sign and, in some cases, a bench. To address liability issues, the following is noted on the sign:

> Drivers don't have to take the first in line;
> You're not obliged to accept a ride, that's fine.
> You accept a ride at your own risk,
> But the ride is free, so consider it a gift.

The aim was to provide an alternative to single-occupancy cars, reducing greenhouse gas emissions and traffic congestion. The car stops are entirely voluntary; people take rides and give lifts as they see fit. Hans, a new resident of Pender Island, describes some of his experiences using the car stops:

> I was hitching a ride using the car-stop system when it had just been recently established on Pender Island. As our family car is of-

ten in my wife's possession, the car stops offered me a way to get around. But being new on the island, I was initially hesitant to use them. Before long, however, I was hooked.... They are a wonderful way to meet people. I have been picked up by construction workers, lawyers, retirees, young and old, rich and poor. Their vehicles have ranged from a luxurious Mercedes SUV to trucks to old heaps held together by duct tape.

I seldom wait more than three cars, and once aboard we chat about the approaching fall fair, water shortages, recent infestations of raccoons and rats on the island, and local gossip.

Once, a small red car stopped. The driver, a little white-haired lady who could barely see over the top of the steering wheel, beckoned me to get in. Turning to her companion, another elderly lady, she asked with a mischievous grin, "Do you think we'll be safe with him?" "I hope not," giggled her friend.

Barry says there has been a change in who uses the car stops. At first, it was mostly students and boaters who used them, not seniors or others who usually drove their cars. "Little by little that pattern has broken down," he says. "There has been a culture shift, and there's now a feeling on the island that it is okay to give people lifts and it is okay to receive them." Different stories in transformative spaces are changing the culture.

Transformative Space

While there has been a culture shift regarding giving and receiving lifts on Pender Island, the car stops are still part of the car culture, which is one of the primary contributors to greenhouse gas emissions. The question arises, with this initiative and others deeply embedded within the current system, does it make sense to have transition initiatives that tinker with the edges of the existing system rather than full system change? Robb gives us his thoughts on this:

Once you have a different mode of thinking, you can either create a new system or you can shift the existing system. You can use the new way of thinking in the old system, and in some cases that's effective or efficient. A lot of times it's efficient because there's such a huge infrastructure built up. So, we're going to get rid of all the cars, but we're going to keep all those roadways because they're great bike pathways. We're not going to tear out all the roadways and then make new bike paths.

upon reflection   The shift to ecological rather than economic thinking is not a straightforward one. Transition options can be a pathway towards an alternative system. They acknowledge that we are often wavering between two ways of being, with dominant culture stories still embedded in our decision-making, even after that flip to a different mode of thinking. And for those who have not shifted their mode of thinking, something like a car stop experience might introduce a new storyline into their consciousness.

Velo-village

John Rowlandson is working with others to shift Salt Spring Islanders towards a cycling culture. From his perspective, "we want to strengthen and deepen cycling culture on Salt Spring." So, when the international cycling conference, Velo-city, was coming to Vancouver he approached them and suggested a Velo-village conference for Salt Spring Island that would focus on rural cycling. Moreover, he engaged unrelated parts of Salt Spring society in the project. The artists hosted a pART project, producing a range of art pieces that depicted and used various bicycle parts. For example, one artist produced a mobile, composed of The Spin Decoder, The Muzzle By-Pass, and The Bitumen Eater. The first bicycle-only BC Ferries crossing from Vancouver Island to Salt Spring Island was another part of Velo-village.

School children decorated older bikes that organizers provided. One of the teachers described the process: "They brought four bikes for us, and we're going to be painting them up and giving them back, so the kids have already brainstormed what they want to do with their bikes—they have their different ideas—so one will be a rainbow unicorn bike, the others a Salt Spring hippy bike, a random recycle bike, and a light bike."

In addition, the invitation went out to other small communities throughout British Columbia and beyond. Over 1,500 cyclists showed up at the cycling event, and Salt Spring Island had more bikes than cars on the road for a brief period in time. Does that one- or two-day period produce culture change? John believes that it gives people insight into the potential for a cycle rather than car culture.

We want to demonstrate what it looks like—if we can bring 1,500 cyclists here over the three days, there's a good chance that most of them will be riding a bike rather than driving a car, right? And so, when people ask, "What do we need to do to make this a more cycle-friendly community where cars are not as dominant?" they just need to be standing in town by the 1,000-bike parking lot, which will take up about 1/10th of the space that 1,000 cars would.

His aim is to shift the culture to shift the system, "We want to strengthen and deepen cycling culture on Salt Spring."

upon reflection Sometimes compassion sounds a lot like common sense. When you imagine yourself walking in someone else's shoes (how appropriate for transportation!) you realize that tearing up roads to make cycling paths, or creating a no-car community because that's what you feel should happen, may not work for others who haven't decided to go without fossil fuel cars. Providing people with opportunities to celebrate bikes or use car stops not only carries inspiration beyond the initial excitement, it empowers other people to rethink their transportation modes, without a lecture or inconvenience in sight. Creating the new society while the old one is still there lets people choose without feeling judged.

The Gertie bus service

Why don't we use waste vegetable oil to help fuel a bus system on Gabriola?!!!

During a recent week, 396 people, four dogs, and a rooster took trips on Gertie, Gabriola's community bus. There's a good chance that none of those creatures realized just how much work had gone into making their bus trip a reality!

Gertie began about ten years ago. Judith and Fay were both interested in alternatives to car culture and keen to see the island reduce its greenhouse gas emissions. In that conversation, they imagined a bus fueled by waste vegetable oil (WVO) as a way to achieve several goals all at once. They joined forces with Deb, another islander, who had also been promoting the idea of a bus as part of taking action on climate change.

What followed was a wonderful example of a community organizing to support a project.

A community meeting, sponsored by the local ratepayer's organization, gathered about twenty islanders who supported the project. By coincidence, British Columbia residents had just received what the provincial government called a Climate Change Dividend of $100, and the bus group (now with a fourth core member) decided on a fundraising campaign that asked people to donate this dividend, or what they could afford, to help fund the bus. About $5,000 was raised, representing 500 island residents who were willing to put their money where their enthusiasm was.

They had to be patient! The gestation period was over five years. For the members of the organizing committee, it was a busy time. There were surveys and studies and route planning and bus shopping and a lot of work to comply with regulations of all kinds. There were conversations with other small communities with bus systems, and trips to biodiesel and alternative transit conferences. And there were regulators. To carry passengers in Canada, bus operators must satisfy several regulators. Funding for two of the original buses came from a fund administered by a level of local government; the application process for that also took a lot of effort and energy.

Through it all, the community was involved. The name-the-bus competition was especially popular. Fay recounts the story:

spiral of change

> We had over 150 names submitted from the community. We went through two rounds of voting and ended up with G.E.R.T.I.E.— Gabriola's Environmentally Responsible, Trans-Island Express. Community members felt ownership of the bus system because they had been part of the naming.
>
> They named the bus system; they named the buses; they came out to celebrate our birthday; they came out to celebrate our launch.... People were engaged. People felt it was their bus. We went for a $10,000 BC Hydro Champions award—an online contest for community groups, sponsored by the provincial electrical utility—and everyone was voting. The whole island joined in, and I think that is where the real strength came from—that voting. Whether it was voting for a name or voting for the $10,000, people were engaged. People were making up songs about Gertie!

The community support continued when the pilot project ended. Fay continues:

> So after three years we went for a referendum, so that the bus drivers would begin to get paid, and we got 67 or 68 percent, or something like that. So now we're a taxpayer-funded bus system. But we're still a community bus system!

Looking back, Fay is a little surprised that there was some negative reaction when the referendum was launched. That was outweighed by the positive, though.

People offering to sing for us at benefit concerts, people creating songs, the volunteer drivers, even people volunteering to filter the waste vegetable oil.... The excitement about Gertie, the way Gertie made people feel like they could do things.... You know I never imagined, "This is what is going to happen if we do this." But it did.

To ponder

Reflect on your community. What are the primary transportation modes in your community, your region, or your country? What actions have people and businesses taken to reduce their fossil-fuel vehicle use in your community? Is it easy for cyclists to get around? Is it easy for people to walk from home to work, from home to events, services, and groceries? Is your shopping area designed for cars or people? How are learning and knowledge about transportation use being transferred within your community, as well as between your community and others across the continent and beyond? Have government agencies responded to the culture shift within communities with any policy changes or initiatives? How have your personal transportation habits shifted as you learned different stories about transportation and reflected on them through compassion, wisdom, and practice?

There is No Away

Spirals and cross purposes

 Thinking about Waste

"Waste" is both a noun and a verb. As a noun, it sounds innoc-
uous enough: just material that is not wanted or that is no longer needed after a process is complete. As a verb, the definitions
sound more sinister: "to use or expend carelessly, extravagantly,
or to no purpose" (Oxford); "the action of spending or using carelessly or uselessly" (Merriam-Webster). It's the first meaning,
waste as a noun, that we'll focus on now.

Waste is different from the things we talk about in the other
chapters. Food, shelter, and transportation are all necessities for
survival, and each requires the use of energy. We can change the
choices we make about each of them, but we can't eliminate them
from our lives—we can't "not have" them. At the same time, the
choices we make—particularly in food, shelter, and transportation—are important for reasons far beyond survival, as demonstrated in the preceding chapters. Waste isn't quite like that. It is
a by-product of living that must be dealt with rather than a necessity for survival. Our choices around waste are not immediately
obvious to those we meet. Images of an extravagant lifestyle—the

kind we may see reflected in movies or glossy magazines—don't include waste at all.

In our everyday lives, we talk about throwing things "away" as if there really was an "away" to throw things to. On our finite planet, that has never been true. In some traditional cultures the composition of waste was different than it is in our industrialized world. First Nations cultures in Canada traditionally shared a principle that it was appropriate to take only what was needed for living and for ceremonial purposes. Since everything that was taken was from the natural world, the waste involved was composed of barely transformed natural fibers. In the coastal regions of the Pacific Northwest, there are many archaeological sites that primarily contain the shells of clams, oysters, and mussels. In other sites animal bones, broken tools, and other objects also appear, all made of the things of the earth and slowly returning to it.

Early settlers were reluctant to waste anything, but for somewhat different reasons. Manufactured objects were expensive, especially things shipped over great distances. In most homes, saving money to provide security for the future would have been a higher priority than purchasing an object. Durable objects were not treated lightly. Furniture and other items were re-used and repaired when necessary. As late as World War II, this idea prevailed. A poster from the era exhorted people to "Use it up, wear it out, make it do," rather than wasting manufactured items and thus diverting materials from the war effort. (The very existence of this poster suggests, though, that a shift from traditional frugality with materials had begun.)

The 1950s saw the rise of consumer culture in North America, with an increased acceptance of so-called "disposable" items not designed to last. More long-distance shipping meant increased packaging, which becomes waste as soon as its primary task is complete. Manufactured products tend to be constructed of multiple materials and, like packaging, tend to become waste when they are no longer suitable for their original purpose. Increased use of plastics has led to the production of new and more problematic forms of waste: to create plastics we create molecules that never existed in nature, and thus there is no natural process that re-uses them.

Waste can mean many things: the obvious truckloads of garbage hauled to landfills, the human energy devoted to creating unnecessary things, and often the things themselves. Waste in almost all its manifestations contributes to the production of greenhouse gases and, hence, climate change. In the USA, the Environmental Protection Agency estimates that every person discards between four and five pounds of garbage per day. In Canada, according to the Recycling Council of British Columbia, every individual produces a bit more than that: 2.7 kilograms (5.9 pounds).

What can we do about it? The question can seem as overwhelming as the piles and piles of garbage headed for those landfills. While we will touch on other types of waste in this interlude, we'll dig deep into how clothing contributes to the waste stream. Its manufacturing, useful life, and disposal reflect many problems with waste of all types, and it is something familiar to all of us. We need it to stay warm, dry, and safe. We use it to communicate. Our clothes tell other people something about our work, our aspirations, and the kind of people we are. We don't often look at the processes needed to get that clothing to us, from the extraction of finite raw materials to the disposal of unwanted garments. Although the city of Vancouver estimates that the approximately 98 tonnes (108 US tons) of textiles that end up in their landfill represent just 1 percent of solid waste by volume, this is an important example, partly because it is so close to home.

Clothing

In this era of "fast fashion," global clothing production doubled between 2000 and 2014. That's a lot of fabric! On average, people keep their clothing only about half as long as they did 15 years ago. Making and mending isn't as popular as it was in the past, perhaps because it seems less necessary; a quick walk through your local shopping centre will remind you that we are expected to want what's new, and that new clothing is often very inexpensive. The shopping centre is designed to make it all seem so easy, but away from the mall there are many ways in which clothing contributes to the waste stream, both before and after purchase.

Let's begin with manufacturing. The production of a kilogram of fabric produces about 23 kilograms of greenhouse gases. This is partly because of the type of fabric that is most common. A quick check of the tags on all those new clothes brings us to polyester, a manufactured material made of polymers (long-chain molecules) derived from petroleum. A lot of energy is required to transform petroleum into fabric.

"But," you say, "I use natural cotton." Unfortunately, cotton is not the energy-innocent alternative it might seem. As a commercial crop, cotton survives through the application of insecticides and other chemicals. A couple of ounces of chemicals are typically used to grow the cotton for a single t-shirt, unless the cotton is grown organically. And although organic cotton is increasingly available, the top producers are India, Turkey, and China, meaning that it is shipped a long way before it gets to North America. Dyeing fibers causes still more waste. The dyeing process uses a lot of water; this waste water contains dyes that can persist in the environment for years.

There's more to the waste than what happens in the manufacturing process, both before and after manufacturing. In our finite world, the materials for manufacturing must come from somewhere on the planet. A 2017 report from the Ellen MacArthur Foundation sums up the problems:

> The current system for producing, distributing, and using clothing operates in an almost completely linear way. Large amounts of nonrenewable resources are extracted to produce clothes that are often used for only a short period, after which the materials are largely lost to landfill or incineration. It is estimated that more than half of fast fashion produced is disposed of in under a year. This linear system leaves economic opportunities untapped, puts pressure on resources, pollutes and degrades the natural environment and its ecosystems, and creates significant negative societal impacts at local, regional, and global scales.

Post-production, the problems continue. Many discarded clothes end up in landfill. In some areas, curbside recycling programs include fabric. This seems to be becoming less common rather than more, possibly because of the difficulty of recycling modern garments. Many garments blend multiple fabrics: the polyester lining in your wool coat likely means that the components must be separated before they can be recycled. There is also growing concern about microfibers, the tiny synthetic threads released when clothing is washed. Many of these fibers are too small to be removed by water treatment plants, and many of them enter rivers and ultimately oceans.

Even our efforts to re-use and recycle can cause unanticipated problems. The organization WhyDev explored the impact of second-hand clothing donations globally. Donated clothing is often shipped in bales to less wealthy nations. These exports help contribute to North American trade surpluses and to the trade deficits of other nations. (In our economic system a trade surplus is better for the economy than a deficit). Clothes shipped overseas are kept out of our landfills, but the arrival of cheap clothing in local markets disrupts local clothing industries, transforming clothing from something someone makes locally to something everyone buys.

Other "stuff"

Because local governments are responsible for the creation and maintenance of landfills, they pay a lot of attention to the garbage we all throw "away" each year. (In a well-managed landfill, "away" really isn't going anywhere. Since waste is buried, there is little decomposition.) What's in them? Organics are often the largest category; hence, the many recent local government programs for food recycling and diversion of yard waste. Paper products make up a large percentage. In North America, plastics seem to hover at around 15 percent of the solid waste stream. Other substantial categories include what is sometimes called "household hygiene" (including diapers and pet waste), wood, and glass. The organic waste category includes food waste, and there is lots of that.

Canadians waste $31 billion worth of food each year, according to the Value Change Management center; Americans waste about $160 billion, according to figures quoted in *The Atlantic*.

Any of these substances used to manufacture the stuff we buy could be the focus of a whole other chapter. Our economic system is based on the production and disposal of things. Our economies are huge. So much is manufactured, and through all these processes there is waste.

 ## Changemakers' Waste Stories

In the chapter on waste we hear some stories about products created from waste. We hear how Mary and Robbie use a composting toilet, not only to produce useful compost but also to lessen their water use requirements. We hear the story of how the Hornby free store started and influenced other communities to communally recycle and re-use, and we hear about the Dirty Mothers Clothing Swap. We explore the exciting world of upcycling clothing, and the connection between cleaning products and waste vegetable oil.

Composting toilets

Robbie remembers reading a book called *Goodbye to the Flush Toilet* in the mid-'70s. "My sister Jackie…always laughed and said, 'Oh, it's that book about not flushing your toilet.' It basically went through the arguments in favor of finding alternatives to the flush toilet." As a result of reading the book Robbie and Mary were converted to the concept of composting toilets. "In the 1970s toilets used five gallons of water per flush, and low-flush ones used three gallons…a *lot* of water."

Robbie and Mary were in their twenties at the time and didn't own property so it wasn't until the '90s that they started implementing the concept. Their story epitomizes the spiral of learning: two steps forward, one back, more experimentation, frustration, and finally a solution that works for them. It also highlights the regulatory challenges inherent in something that no one really wants to talk about—human waste.

> *Our first was an installed [commercial] one.... We were building our house in '95 and we were very concerned about having the smallest footprint we could for that house. The waste we were trying to avoid was, first, the waste of money and time required to buy materials to build space the two of us really didn't need and, second, the waste of water. So we really wanted to go with a composting toilet. We wanted to do water collection and not do a well. We didn't know much about building your own toilet at that point so we bought a unit. Also, we wanted to comply with zoning requirements.*

However, the local regulations weren't all that obvious when it came to composting toilets. As Mary explains,

> *It wasn't that clear that we could do it at first. We put composting toilet on the plan, and everyone threw their hands in the air. The planning department said, "It has nothing to do with us because it's a toilet." And then the health department said, "It has nothing to do with us because it's not hooked up to the sewer." So nobody was going to approve it. At the same time, someone had to, so they finally concluded that it was okay as long as we put in the rest of the septic system. But the conversation around that took quite a while.*

On the Gulf Islands, as in many rural areas throughout North America, there is no public sewage system. Any building with a toilet—be it a house, a business, a school or anything else—must be built with a way of disposing of human wastes and wastewater. In almost all cases, this means a septic tank and field system. In this kind of system, waste all goes into a buried tank. From there, it flows out into a series of perforated pipes buried in the soil in an area that is left undisturbed (usually seeded to grass). About 25 percent of homes in North America use this type of system, according to *Wikipedia*. The systems are fairly low maintenance (tanks need to be pumped occasionally) and the expected life of the system is approximately 50 years.

This approach is in line with North American responses to human waste. Those attitudes can be pretty much summed up in one word—eeewwww! The tank and field system, like urban waste treatment systems, focuses on getting the waste out of sight and to that magical place where all unwanted things go—"away."

In their current house, Mary and Robbie went through three iterations of composting toilet before settling on their current system, which they love. They tried another commercial composting toilet. "It was expensive, and used even more water. It had a 12 volt battery and was a very, very fancy vacuum flush unit. The toilet was inside and the vacuum flush went to the composter outside. The composter outside wasn't big enough so Robbie built a bigger compost box." However, their experience of this system was "horrible."

Then Robbie discovered the *Humanure Handbook* by Joseph Jenkins. "We built that and it works a treat." In this system, a bucket containing a few inches of wood shavings is contained in a wooden box with a toilet seat on top. An extraction fan carries odors outside to a chimney. Wood chips are added per use. The bucket is then emptied into a large compost pile.

> It does everything it says it does. It makes so much sense to me when I see a big compost pile. The compost pile he recommends is five feet square and about three feet high. There's no odor to it. And it's hot. I've used a thermometer on it and check continuously. And it sometimes gets down to 100 degrees and if it ever gets below 100 then I know something's gone wrong. Normally it is sitting at about 110 and in hot summer weather sometimes it will bounce up to about 125. That's a cooking compost, that's too hot to put your hand into it.

And Mary adds—"It's cooking…it's cooking pathogens." The health fear regarding composting toilets is that the compost won't get hot enough to kill the pathogens. At 110°F (43°C) the humanure compost pile is more than capable of doing the job. This was their second humanure compost bin. They originally built a smaller bin that worked but didn't get quite as hot as their final version. Each experiment taught them something more about what works best.

They fill one box, then leave the contents to finish composting and age for a year while they use the other box. They use the compost as a top dressing on their fruit trees and blueberries.

They love the system, are never short of water when neighbors are having to truck water in to fill cisterns, and their trees and bushes are getting added nutrients. So, why aren't more people doing it?

> We're surprised it hasn't caught on, because out here in the summer people are always suffering so much with their wells going dry and shortage of water. Our primary motivation was not so much about using the human waste as about not wasting water. When you think about the city and all of the water treatment that goes on so that we can flush our toilets with drinking water it just seems absurd.
>
> Even out here, you've got to get the water out of the well, right, and then in the summer your well is going dry, and yet you have to throw good water into your septic field. You're taking it out of the immediate source of availability and that just seems kind of crazy. And the combination of composting toilet and rainwater collection just seems to make sense.

They then answered their own query about why more people weren't putting in composting toilets: "There's something about squeamishness. We've had people come to the house here who are clearly shaken by it: 'There's something in the toilet.' Yeah, it's a sawdust toilet. You have to pee in the sawdust."

Yet in many parts of the world (and in some areas of North America too, to be fair) human excreta is valued for agricultural use.

There are two types of composting toilets: aerobic, and anaerobic. The humanure system that Robbie and Mary use is aerobic. Robbie explains:

The aerobic bacteria generate heat, and that heat keeps the process going. The other [system] is the anaerobic digester, which is also absolutely brilliant. The anaerobic bacteria need a hot temperature to keep the system going—they don't generate it themselves. In the tropics an anaerobic system makes total sense. In India they have a whole department devoted to it. They're cheap, and you can put it in on a village-size scale and they generate fuel. Some people have calculated that a family generates enough fuel to cook its food for the day.

A number of people have been interested in their composting toilet, and some people have built their own as a result of experiencing the one in Mary and Robbie's house. There have also been various discussions in the broader community about building more composting toilets and changing the regulations to make it an option rather than an addition to the traditional septic and treatment systems.

Perhaps the biggest step is being able to talk about it—to turn it from the "eeewwww" topic to a topic about the uses and benefits. As Mary, Robbie and composting toilet systems across the world have demonstrated, when we acknowledge our unmentionable waste it can lead to less water use, compost, and even fuel to cook our food.

Hornby Island Free Store

In the late 1960s, Hornby Island was a tiny community with a population of fewer than 200 people. The island is a little challenging to get to. You take a ferry from Vancouver Island to Denman Island, then drive across Denman and take another ferry to Hornby. The closest small city is Courtenay, which is about a 15-minute drive from the ferry landing on Vancouver Island.

Like most tiny communities, Hornby Island had a garbage dump. Shelagh moved to Hornby in 1969, and the way she describes it, this was a dump in the classic sense—an area where everyone hauled their own garbage and dumped it. There was no garbage collection, so if people wanted to make a different choice, they would have had to load up a truck, take the two ferries, and take their garbage to Courtenay's dump. Most didn't. When the population was very small, this seemed okay. Beginning in the late 1960s, the population began to grow rapidly. The dump became more and more of a mess, with rats and other pests and smelly problems.

The island's new arrivals, like Shelagh, were mostly young back-to-the-landers and craftspeople, most with very little money but with a willingness to do things themselves. Many were building their own homes, and they were happy to use salvaged lumber and other materials. Some of these things could be found in the dump, where others had thrown them away. Hornby's new approach to waste, one that has been emulated in many other small communities, began, as Shelagh says, with the idea that "if you take something to the dump that someone else can use, don't just chuck it in the rain." Community members built a set of sheds just to keep re-usable things moderately dry, and that was the beginning. Shelagh describes how the dump became more and more organized as the years went on, becoming more official, with support from the Hornby Island Residents and Ratepayers Association, and eventually being recognized by the Regional District (the rather distant local authority for such matters) as a fundable local approach to the problem of solid waste.

"Almost anything we could have done would have been economically more viable than the alternative," Shelagh says, and that's partly why it worked. Hornby's isolation led to local innovation, and the cost of trucking garbage encouraged government agencies to support the innovation. (Or, as Shelagh puts it, the Regional District likely realized that letting the hippies do it would save them money.)

In 1978 the Hornby Island recycling depot was officially launched, and Kathi became the coordinator. Kathi describes the rationale behind the center on the Hornby Island Residents' and Ratepayers' Association (HIRRA) website:

The motivation for the island to try recycling was economic and I applied for the job for economical reasons too. I didn't want to see all that useful "stuff" shipped off the island and become inaccessible. Where would we go to find a tail light for our vehicle or a damper for the stove, or a curtain rod, or...? There was little space at the Co-op for hardware, trips to town were infrequent, and if your neighbor didn't have what you needed, there was always "the dump," a great resource for all kinds of things. Here was a chance to organize other people's garbage into something useful to someone else and to keep our stuff out of someone else's landfill.

The Recycling Center has continued to evolve in its almost forty years of operation, and it's made it possible for Hornby to recycle up to 70 percent of the waste residents generate. It's also been an inspiration to other small communities in British Columbia and beyond. The old landfill is capped now, and there's a garden on top. At one time garbage was incinerated, but that practice was stopped in 1991, and garbage is now hauled off the island. Glass and tin are still recycled, just as in 1978, but now so are plastics, batteries, metal, and a host of other things. One of the most popular parts of the center is the Free Store, beloved by island residents and visitors alike. The Free Store, and its sense of an ongoing treasure hunt for clothes, household items, and anything you could possible imagine, helps Hornby be sure that things that are not needed don't become waste.

Challenging fast fashion—the Dirty Mothers, upcycling, and building community

As the Hornby Free Store illustrates, there are plenty of ways to reduce the need for new clothing, keep older clothes in circulation, and avoid the waste that comes with fast fashion. Clothing swaps among friends, especially popular with parents of young children, are another way. And then there are clothing swaps with a difference, like the Dirty Mothers Clothing Swap.

Sue first learned about Dirty Mother Clothing Swaps in Prince Edward Island, when she lived there and was active in the women's movement in the 1970s and '80s.

> *I thought it was absolutely brilliant for a number of reasons. One was that it was a great way to refresh your wardrobe without spending any money. And it was a great way to not waste stuff. In addition, it was community building. It was a great chance to socialize with folks that I often don't get together with very often.*

This was a clothing swap, designed not just to share clothing but to build community. Sue introduced the swaps on Gabriola, and she describes a twice-yearly ritual that developed around the events, complete with hand-drawn notices and a ritual bottle of tequila.

> *Everyone would bring all their gear in black plastic bags, and we'd empty them out into a great heap in the middle of the room. I had a whistle, and at a certain point I'd blow the whistle and everyone would dive in. Some of my most favorite clothes have come from Dirty Mothers over the years.*

Why Dirty Mothers? That's all part of the ritual. A Dirty Mother is a drink, traditionally made with a mixture of Kahlua, tequila, and cream. Each clothing swap begins with the participants spending time together, enjoying a drink (or not—it's not compulsory) and eyeing the tempting pile of garments. Once the whistle blows, the action is swift!

Sue notes that the swaps don't have to be for women only. For her groups, that has been the most comfortable, since it allows for immediate try-ons and encourages modelling of good scores. The best-organized swaps are set up with a place in mind, in advance, to send anything that is not claimed—on Gabriola they've variously gone on to the local recycle center or to local quilters for the fabric.

"Dirty Mothers can contribute to a more sane, humane, and ecological future," Sue concludes.

Fighting fast fashion one garment at a time

Doreen knows all about fast fashion. In fact, her business card says "Fighting Fast Fashion One Garment at a Time." She is a talented seamstress and designer and an upcycler. She takes clothes that people have discarded, or much-loved sweaters that have met with disaster in the form of a stain or a moth-hole, and transforms them into unique garments. As Doreen says,

> What I try to do is to fight fast fashion with green fashion. Pre-existing textiles are the greenest textiles there are. We don't need to process them.... The only thing we need to do is wash them.

Avoiding waste is a big part of Doreen's concerns. She knows about the pounds of clothing thrown out every year by Canadians (68 pounds per person, according to her research) and is continually shocked by the volume of clothing donations at the Gabriola recycling depot. Waste isn't her only concern. She speaks passionately about the working conditions of those who make fabric; many are debt-indentured or even slaves, and working conditions are often appalling. She also sees the stress that ordinary people are under in daily life, and the way that many people seem to use shopping as an escape from stress. She sees upcycling as one way to fight back against the interlocking systems involved.

> Corporations spend billions a year trying to figure out ways to get us to keep purchasing, and purchasing as much as we can, and carrying the biggest debt loads we are willing to. One way they do that is fast fashion. We used to have four seasons.... Now we have 52. There are stores in the malls that promise every time you come in, we will have new stuff. But you wash it three times and it loses its shape and its color.... It is not going to be re-usable.

For Doreen upcycling isn't just about doing the right thing for other people, though. It's also about creating a more enjoyable life and wearing clothes that represent the wearer.

> Upcycling—t-shirts and jeans are boring. Boring! I can't tell you! It is not infrequent that I will open up a bag at GIRO [Gabriola

*Island Recycling Organization] and there will be four t-shirts or
tops, all the same but different colors.... I think BORING! Okay, it's
easy to get dressed in the morning,...but isn't it just as easy to get
dressed in an interesting way?*

*People will throw out 100 percent marino sweaters or cash-
mere because of stretching or a moth hole or coffee.... You can
cut them up and put them together in a different way to get
something really unique.*

*upon
reflection*   There's a sense of excitement and discovery to free
stores, to clothing swaps, and to upcycling. The discovery is never going to be just another boring t-shirt! Yet we may
still find ourselves seeking the new rather than the used or up-
cycled. To really weave these initiatives into the web of daily life,
they need to become preferred options, ones that can both provide ways of keeping useful resources out of the waste stream
and reduce our cost of living.

Fueled by waste vegetable oil

Using waste vegetable oil for fueling buses would seem to be a
win-win story. Restaurants don't have to pay someone to cart
waste vegetable oil out of the community in large emission-
producing trucks. The oil is used to produce a fuel that costs less
than fossil fuels and doesn't produce the greenhouse gas emissions that diesel or gas produce. Yet, trying to make it happen created waves on Gabriola Island.

Judith, Fay, and Bob wanted to convert the waste vegetable oil
produced by island restaurants into biodiesel for the community
bus. They applied for and received a grant to hire a summer student from the alternative energy program at the local college to
research the process and assess the viability of creating biodiesel
on Gabriola Island.

Working with Bob, Lisa (the student) produced a report that
described the various do-it-yourself, as well as commercial,

processors and corresponding processes. She visited a large biodiesel cooperative in a neighboring region and analyzed the amount of waste vegetable oil produced on Gabriola, to determine the most appropriate batch size. She talked to the various restaurants and pubs, and they loved the idea that their waste vegetable oil would be used for fueling the buses on the island, rather than being shipped outside the community.

However, the team bumped up against some opposition. When Lisa did a demonstration on the creation of biodiesel at the Fall Fair, a representative of the company that was currently picking up waste vegetable oil from the restaurants heckled her. Several community members spread a rumor that glycerin (a product of biodiesel production) attracts rats when composted and is harmful to the soil. The final criticism was that the biodiesel processing was dangerous and could blow up. These concerns were not usually communicated directly to the team working on the project; instead they were communicated by word of mouth, over the backyard fence, and the criticisms spread. The organizers decided not to proceed until the concerns had been addressed.

A couple of years later two of the organizers attended a biodiesel conference and heard how mixing diesel with the waste vegetable oil mix provides an alternative to making biodiesel from the waste vegetable oil. After further research and input from community members, the community bus group decided to combine filtered waste vegetable oil with diesel and use that mix for fueling the community bus. There were no protests from the community, and the company that had initially been against the community's use of WVO from the restaurants had lost interest in protesting since all the restaurants were much happier keeping it on the island to fuel the bus. Gertie, the community bus, was fueled by the WVO and diesel mixture for over four years.

However, during those four years there were various opinions about whether or not the waste vegetable oil was harming the elaborate fuel injection systems on two of the vehicles. Debates about the pros and cons of using the WVO/diesel mixture occurred between those looking after the mechanical side of the buses, those focused on reducing greenhouse gas emissions, and those driving the vehicles. In the end, there was a decision to proceed with fueling two of the vehicles with the mix, and the other two, which had more sensitive fueling systems, were fueled with diesel while biodiesel was being reconsidered.

Island Futures, the organization that had sponsored the original report, stepped up. Recognizing all of the original criticisms, they started producing the biodiesel in a locked area to address the safety concerns, and they used the glycerin by-product to make liquid soap rather than composting it.

Cross Purposes to a Wheel in Motion

upon reflection   There are numerous examples of cross purposes in this story. Turning waste vegetable oil into fuel was one purpose, another was ensuring children were safe; another was preventing rats from overrunning the community; and yet another was to hold on to a job transporting the waste vegetable oil. The challenge was to find ways to work with all the cross purposes and come up with solutions that everyone felt addressed their particular goal.

Is it root beer?

"It looks like Maple Syrup."

"Is it root beer?"

"It's a by-product of biodiesel? Does that mean it's got diesel in it?"

"The color puts me off."

"The smell is weird. It just doesn't smell like soap."

"It worked so well as a shampoo!"

"I used it on my grill—cleaned it right up. Couldn't believe it. It's great."

"We used it for a deep clean in the community kitchen—it was amazing! It cleaned every greasy surface without a problem!"

"It's going to be our go-to Christmas gift for everyone."

The preceding comments are all about the liquid soap produced out of the glycerin by-product from the biodiesel-making operation. Fay produced the soap from the glycerin, put it into recycled dish soap containers, named it Glean, and sold it at the farmers market.

After a close friend mentioned that he missed the peppermint smell of the soap that he used, Fay added peppermint oil to some of the containers. Many who had been hesitant due to the neutral smell of the original bought the peppermint soap, while others remained true to the unscented soap.

There were challenges from people who weren't willing to let go of stories about what soap looks like: "It's brown! I couldn't even imagine cleaning something with that." There was also a positive resonance from those using it: "This is perfect. It's from recycled waste vegetable oil; it's a waste product from the biodiesel; I can recycle the container—and it cleans everything! The perfect recycling circle!"

upon reflection   Both the biodiesel processing and the creation of Glean were initiated by three people seeing waste from a different perspective. A small group of concerned citizens is how shifts begin. Most recently, conversations are beginning on Gabriola Island about creating a plastic-bag-free shopping experience. Many other communities have taken similar steps, banning plastic bags and water bottles, and a small group is continuing discussions on Gabriola.

As with so many other stories, this initiative begins with a single individual or tiny group deciding that a practice in their community does not align with their values. In Concord, Massachusetts, for example, Public Radio International (PRI) reports that plastic water bottles were banned in response to an initiative led by 88-year-old Jean Hill. She was inspired by her eight-year-old grandson, who had learned about plastic pollution in the ocean and shared what he knew. "He said, 'You know, Grandma, there are big things circling around in the water that are as big as Texas, and they're full of plastic trash,' and I finally realized that these gyres, these circular currents, are full of plastic," Hill says. "And there's a fish called a lanternfish that eats bits of plastic that then get into the food chain," she explains." The concerns of individuals, acted upon, can have a big impact.

To ponder

Reflect on your community. How much waste is created per person in your community, your region, or your country? What actions have people and businesses taken to reduce waste in your community? Are there examples of upcycling or turning waste into something useful for your community? How is learning and knowledge about reducing waste being transferred within your community, as well as between your community and others across the continent and beyond? Have government agencies responded to the culture shift in communities with any policy changes or initiatives? For example, is there a composting program? How have your personal waste habits shifted as you learned different stories about waste through compassion, wisdom, and practice?

People Power

The neighborhood effect

 Thinking about Energy

Fossil fuel energy is used to operate the dominant culture. In Canada, in 2013, the percentage of energy used for significant systems was as follows: industry 28 percent, transportation 21 percent, residential 12 percent, commercial and institutional 7 percent, and agriculture 2 percent. Producing the energy consumed was the other 30 percent. In 2014, Canada's production of primary energy included crude oil (43 percent) and natural gas (33 percent). Biomass, wind, tidal, and solar made up 4 percent.

Over 84 percent of our energy production is from fossil fuels, which are non-renewable sources of energy. Oil, gas, and coal that were formed millions of years ago from the remains of plants and animals are now becoming depleted and more difficult to extract. The extraction and use of fossil fuels in the past century has resulted in demand threatening to outstrip supply. Potential responses include paying the higher cost involved in extracting those fossil fuels that are difficult or more energy intensive to extract (oil sands, deep sea sources), increasing the renewable sources, reducing energy use, or a combination of the above. While there is evidence of all four responses in government and mainstream media communication, the current focus in Canada is on paying the higher cost—for example, Alberta's tar sands.

In addition to the likelihood that we will soon run out of cheap fossil fuel, these energy sources create greenhouse gas emissions and harmful particulates when used. For the past two decades the Intergovernmental Panel on Climate Change scientists have been predicting that the current level of greenhouse gas emissions will result in severe weather events and rising sea levels. In May 2012 James Hansen, director of the United States NASA (National Aeronautics and Space Administration) Goddard Institute for Space Studies, wrote an op-ed article in the *New York Times* titled "Game Over for the Planet." He warned,

> *Canada's tar sands...contain twice the amount of carbon dioxide emitted by global oil use in our entire history. If we were to fully exploit this new oil source and continue to burn our conventional oil, gas, and coal supplies, concentrations of carbon dioxide in the atmosphere would reach levels higher than...2.5 million years ago, when sea level was at least 50 feet higher than it is now.... Twenty to 50 percent of the planet's species would be driven to extinction.*
>
> *Over the next several decades...economic losses would be incalculable. More and more of the Midwest would be a dust bowl. California's Central Valley could no longer be irrigated. Food prices would rise to unprecedented levels.*

He describes the interconnection between systems and global relationships. Whether the oil from the tar sands is used in China, the United States, or Canada, the impact will be the same—a concentration of carbon dioxide in the atmosphere that will change the planet. And—just one example of the relationship between global food and energy systems—climate-change-induced drought in California's Central Valley is resulting in reduced access to vegetables and fruits in British Columbia. As noted in the food chapter, 70 percent are currently imported from California.

We have a direct connection to energy use, for example, driving cars or heating residential buildings. We also have an often-forgotten, indirect connection to energy, such as purchasing goods in which energy has been used to extract the resources required, manufacture the product, and then transport it.

 ## Changemakers' Energy Stories

People are responding to the impact of fossil fuel use in many different ways. In this chapter we hear stories about individuals living off the grid, a social enterprise that provides air source heat pumps, another that provides solar panels, energy conservation tools available at a local library, and the implementation of community-owned renewable energy.

Off the electricity grid on Lasqueti Island

While most of the tiny islands that are in the Salish Sea are part of the electricity grid, one of these small islands, Lasqueti, was in line to receive electricity from the large provincial utility (BC Hydro), but they refused. In 1978 BC Hydro attempted to run power lines and use Lasqueti as a stepping stone between the Vancouver area and Vancouver Island. Lasqueti residents did not want the transmission lines. A local politician describes the public meeting with BC Hydro held on Lasqueti:

> At one point or another, the total population attended that meeting. Here is the amazing part: those meetings went on for two solid days, and there were just as many people there during the last hour as on the first day.

The local governments played a support role to the residents, and the proposed route of transmission lines was stopped.

Lasqueti Island residents are still off BC Hydro's grid and use a range of sources for their energy needs, including wood, solar, wind, diesel, and propane. Not having access to either a natural gas or electricity energy grid forces residents on the island to look for alternatives. While some rely on fossil fuel generators for primary or back-up energy others create alternative systems. Philip Vannini describes how one Lasqueti Island resident created an off-the-grid system without a back-up generator:

> *Indeed, building a homestead as a whole is an exercise in choreography. From making the most of a water stream for micro-hydro power to integrating passive solar into a house heating system, building and maintaining an efficient off-grid homestead is like line-dancing with nature and technology.*

Living off the electricity grid requires awareness of each kilowatt of energy used relative to the energy that is available, a consciousness of whether the stream is low or full and generating hydro power, or whether the sun is shining brightly or has been behind clouds for several days. For the resident living on natural sources of energy, the need to understand nature's patterns by putting the theory of alternative energy into practice is crucial.

The notion of working with and understanding nature is evident in some of the previous alternative systems discussed. Alternative food and shelter systems are shifts towards being aware and working with the environment, with one degree of separation from nature rather than multiple degrees.

Mindful Practice

Energy audit lending library

On Bowen Island, you can use your library card to borrow Kill a Watt meters and thermal imaging cameras to determine the energy use and heat loss in your home.

Kim, a Bowen Island resident, decided to get a Kill a Watt meter to find out why her electricity bills were higher than she thought they should be. She plugged the meter in and noted how much energy each appliance used. She then figured out ways to reduce the use of those appliances that were using the most electricity. She learned through practical hands-on experience, just do it.

In conversations with others from Bowen in Transition (a group based on the Transition Town movement) she realized that if others had access to the Kill a Watt meter, they would be able to understand the electrical needs of each of their appliances and, as a result, reduce their energy use more effectively.

So, she talked to the local library about carrying the Kill a Watt meters in the library and they agreed! Bowen in Transition purchased two meters and donated them to the library. As noted in the local paper, "You can borrow the meter with a library card the same way as you would with a book."

Four years later a neighboring organization offered residential energy audits on Bowen Island, and they hired Rod, a local islander, to carry out the audits. He learned how to use a thermal imaging camera to measure temperatures on various surfaces and also to take infrared pictures that show hot and cold spots, both inside rooms and on the outside of buildings.

Using a neighborhood approach, they offered mini audits to a number of homes in the same area. In one of the neighborhoods one of the residents invited all of his neighbors over for a potluck dinner on the day of the audits, and they had a conversation about the results and how they could use the results to start using less energy and reduce heat loss in their homes.

In 2017 Bowen's local government funded the purchase of thermal imaging cameras for Bowen Island, and the public can now check them out at the local library, together with the Kill a Watt meters.

Kim brought this idea to Gabriola when she moved, and the Gabriola library now has two Kill a Watt meters and a thermal imaging camera that can be checked out with a library card.

Living Net

upon reflection Kim provides a clear demonstration of how the living net works. The threads start to spread from the initial sharing with others in her local transition group to a unique collaboration with the library. The opportunity to build on the thermal imaging audits underway creates further threads, and the move to another community creates more again.

Heat pump social enterprise

Of the energy sources used for heating in the Gulf Islands, electricity is one of the lowest in greenhouse gas emissions, as approximately 88 percent of BC Hydro's installed generating capacity is hydroelectric, which has a low direct GHG profile. The remaining 12 percent is fossil fueled and is used for meeting peak demand in winter and supplying remote off-grid locations.

The heat pump social enterprise arose out of a combination of serendipity, government programs, a growing awareness of energy efficiency, financial common sense, and the presence of retirees who wanted to give something back to the community without the need for a paycheck. Chris, a retired telecommunications executive, was advised by a friend that he could get grants that would reduce heat loss from his house if he had an energy audit carried out and then implemented the recommendations. One of those recommendations was the installation of an air-to-air heat pump. He attempted to buy one from a supplier in the city of Nanaimo (20 minutes away by ferry), but they would not sell him one without coming over to the island. In addition, they were going to charge Chris an extra $500 for ferry cost and travel time, whether or not Chris wanted the heat pump. The heat pump itself would cost $5,000.

Chris figured there must be a better way, and after extensive research he found the model that was the most energy efficient. His enthusiasm resulted in two more friends asking him to buy them units. Chris found a wholesaler online and then found a little button on the website that said, "Do you want to be a dealer?" Chris clicked the button and was soon talking to the wholesaler, who, after hearing the story of the Nanaimo supplier and the number of units Chris wanted to order, designated him a dealer. Chris provided the units to his friends at the wholesale cost (approximately $1,700), and, due to reduced heating bills (by up to two thirds in some cases) and government grants, they were able to pay off their heat pumps within a year. The word traveled, as neighbor talked to neighbor, and five years later Chris's "dealership" has provided over 500 heat pumps to island residents.

One of the early purchasers was Bob, a retired engineering professor and also one of the authors of the greenhouse gas emissions and energy audit report for the island. He realized that GHG-reduction benefits would result from the uptake in heat pumps, since electricity was the source for 35 percent of the documented heat generated for buildings on the island (with 47 percent from wood and the rest from fossil fuels). He suggested turning Chris's dealership into a social enterprise by having all purchasers donate $200 to the local sustainability non-profit organization, with the intent that it be directed primarily at reducing energy use on the island, in particular fossil fuels. Both Chris and Bob continue to put hours of volunteer time into supporting the acquisition of heat pumps for islanders; a local resident was hired to install the units, and the non-profit organization has benefitted from the donations.

upon reflection   Patterns from previous examples are also evident in this initiative. As with Lulu's Local, one system change supports shifts in other areas. The heat pumps reduce energy consumption and provide funds for sustainable activities, while Lulu's Local increased local food options while supporting artisans and the arts. Like the car stops' use of the current road and vehicle infrastructure, the heat pump initiative is still part of the purchasing system and electricity grid. Chris used these systems, not to make a profit but rather to provide an alternative way for people and organizations to decrease their energy use.

Solar power

Several Gabriola community members witnessed the success of the heat pump program and decided to try the same approach with solar panels. They registered as a nonprofit society, Gabe Energy, and registered as a wholesaler with one of the solar panel manufacturers. They were able to get a great price on solar panels by buying them in bulk. The Gabriola Commons purchased a 10 kW system; a large farm on the island also installed a 10 kW system; the local Arts Council purchased some for the roof of the Arts Centre; and numerous Gabriola residents took the opportunity to purchase solar panels for their homes. In three years they installed over 28 systems on Gabriola.

People in other communities heard about the program, and the Pender Island Recycling depot, the City of Nelson, and the Hornby Island Free Store installed panels purchased through Gabe Energy, as did organizations in other British Columbia communities. Because setting up systems can feel intimidating to those who have never done it before, Gabe Energy provides assistance in determining the best location and number of units for any of the hardware packages they supply. As a nonprofit society they supply hardware at their wholesale purchase price plus a maximum 12.5 percent administration fee, which includes some system design consultation. Gabe Energy has supplied hardware for a total of 50 systems in BC communities, which equates to 450 kW of electricity produced by solar power.

upon reflection The domino effect described above has been documented elsewhere. Research into solar power in Connecticut demonstrated what researchers called a "neighbor effect," which takes place when a change made by one person inspires others to make the same change. They also noted that, as more people put up solar panels, laws changed to accommodate solar energy, solar power became cheaper due to economies of scale, and it became the social norm to have solar panels. The neighbor effect was also in evidence when Gabe Energy modeled their approach—wholesale plus donation—after the heat pump enterprise.

Power to the community

On Galiano Island a group of people transformed the power of their energy and time into local renewable energy, cooperatively purchased and installed. Tom describes the initial "ah ha" moment:

Where did this start? Basically, it started as an ad hoc group protesting the proposed pipelines. At one point, we found ourselves in a park on Galiano waving placards, and we thought: this is silly, we have to do something other than focus on our adversaries. Going to Vancouver, taking part in a demonstration, and using cars to get over there just seemed counterproductive. What could we do that would be practical and move the conversation along? Why don't we get into solar?

About 30 people from the anti-pipeline group were interested in working on solar systems for the island. Tom had already done about 2½ years of research on solar systems, so that provided a basis for moving forward. He describes the next step: "We divided up the work for what we thought we wanted to do and looked at pricing, feasibility, and so on."

They researched a number of companies that sold solar panels and found out about the necessary permits, along with material and installation costs. Then they decided it was possible and they were going to go for it.

They talked to Dave from Gabe Energy, and he introduced them to the practicalities of setting up solar systems. They traveled by boat up to Gabriola Island, and Dave showed them four different systems that had been set up on Gabriola. One system was off-grid, and three were tied to BC Hydro's grid.

The Galiano group then looked into doing the installation themselves:

> As things were getting a little more serious we hired an electrician on Vancouver Island for a day. There were four of us—as we videoed and recorded everything that he did and demonstrated, we came to realize the size of the task and the steepness of our learning curve. He showed us around to about 12 different systems and we had a 1,000 questions and he had 1,000 answers. By then we knew exactly what we were in for, and we felt that we were practically ready.

At this point the Galiano group had grown to about 65 people, and they were ready to start purchasing systems. In the end 16 systems were ordered. Some were on the ground, some on roofs, some tied to the grid and some not. In total there were 330 modules plus all the components needed. That is almost 80 kWs of power.

Tom describes what happened as neighbors helped neighbors:

> What impressed me was that this idea to go solar actually cut across political lines. The desire for a decarbonized future came together with unhappiness about BC Hydro and coalesced into a community effort to demonstrate the power (and costs) of solar energy. It was quite an interesting and very positive experience.
>
> We had to pick the materials up in Duncan. The local trading company loaned us their truck, and we had to buy insurance and hire a driver. Back on the island, we unloaded 27 tons of equipment into someone's boat shed, got everybody together, and after 2½ hours of sorting the 303 modules, nuts and bolts, and pieces whose importance was discovered later, everything had been distributed. The 27 other modules came later.

They spent the next six months putting them all up, and again it was a community effort. Everybody worked together. According to Tom, "It is so simple to put these up." They still needed an electrician for the final connection for on-grid systems and for the permits through the BC Safety Authority.

They had been thinking of setting up their bulk buying of renewable energy systems as a cooperative to make it more official and easier to manage the financial transactions. They had contacted Vancity (see the Cooperative Economics chapter) prior to their bulk purchase to learn a little bit more about co-ops. Vancity offered support with a business plan and the paperwork required to set up a cooperative. But the Galiano group were so busy putting up solar systems that the co-op idea didn't go anywhere at that point.

However, interest was growing after the initial installment:

So we had a mini workshop on Galiano. By then I had an email list of about 105 people who had very strong interest in this. The CEO of Vancity was in attendance, gave a short presentation on community financing, and encouraged us to pursue the cooperative route in earnest.

They are now waiting for the final changes to the documents to establish themselves as a registered cooperative. They plan to do bulk buys under the cooperative. Looking at the long term, the group decided to go with a for-profit cooperative so that they could, in the future, create a solar farm and work on a power purchase agreement with the provincial utility or choose some other means to support a carbon-free community energy system.

spiral of change

🌿 *upon*
reflection The first steps have been taken towards taking back control of energy in their community. There is a "small group of concerned citizens" that agreed on the need; research was carried out; community members are engaged; 80 kW of solar power is now in place; and a cooperative has formed to create further renewable energy for the community.

Isle of Eigg

Far away from Canada's Gulf Islands sits another small island that has decided to shift away from diesel generators to renewables through the establishment of their own utility. The Isle of Eigg is located in the Hebrides just off the Isle of Skye on the west coast of Scotland. The Island has an interesting history. As described on the Isle of Eigg's Heritage Trust's website,

> After years of instability, neglect, and lack of secure tenure, the Isle of Eigg Heritage Trust was able to purchase the island on 12th June 1997, largely due to the generosity of around ten thousand members of the general public.

The island is only 31 square kilometres (12 square miles), with a population of 83 people. Yet, this small group of islanders decided that they wanted to take ownership of their energy needs. The renewable energy system includes three micro hydro systems with a total of 112 kW, another 50 kW of solar energy, and a 24 kW wind farm, complemented by a battery storage system. The system was financed by Community Energy Scotland and Lottery funds and is managed by Eigg Electric, a community-owned utility, managed and maintained by the residents.

A key component of the system is the agreement among the residents to keep their energy use within certain limits. All the residents signed a commitment to stay under 5 kW of electricity use at any point in time, while businesses signed for under 10 kW. There is also a signal, which they call a "traffic light indicator," that tells people when there is a potential reduction in the power being generated. At that point people reduce their use to less than 4 or 8 kW.

While signing on to restricted energy use could have been a game stopper for the whole system, there was little resistance. One of the residents said, "It just makes sense—and I'm not a strong environmentalist or anything like that." Another resident was enthusiastic and proud: "We pulled it off, much to everyone's surprise."

upon reflection The spirit of "Let's just do it" is evident on the Isle of Eigg. For their electricity system to work, the whole community had to agree to move ahead with it and keep their energy within certain limits. And, on an island known for strong and differing opinions, they all agreed.

To ponder

Reflect on your community. What are the primary energy uses in your community, your region, or your country? What are the primary sources? What actions have people and businesses taken to reduce their energy use and increase the proportion of renewable energy to fossil fuel energy in your community? What is the structure for electrical service—is it a cooperative? How are learning and knowledge about energy use being transferred within your community, as well as between your community and others across the continent and beyond? Have government agencies responded to the culture shift in communities with any policy changes or initiatives? How have your personal energy habits shifted as you learned different stories about energy through compassion, wisdom, and practice?

Cooperative Economics

Making it work for the living net

Thinking about Economics

We cannot come close to adequately providing a "current state of economics." Instead we will provide a brief context for the different stories about economics that follow.

Capitalism is the dominant form of economics in the world in which we live, but it is not the only form. In this very brief description of our current economic system we focus on capitalism but also refer to some of the other forms that are part of our lives, such as cooperatives, social enterprises, caring labor, barter, and the sharing economy.

We will start with the type of capitalism that is wreaking destruction on the environment and on humans. Governments create laws, regulations, and trade agreements that provide corporations with the framework required to function. Rather than the myth of a market free of government intervention, the capitalist system is heavily reliant on the state.

Capitalism has been described as an economic system characterized by property rights, wage labor to produce profits for corporations, and the requirement that officers of a corporation serve the interests of the shareholders—that interest being defined as increasing share values. Capitalism treats environmental impacts from the extraction and use of resources as externalities, with little to no recognition that the environment is a common good and finite.

Corporations can carry out these actions using their rights as "persons" to protect them. The result is private corporations protected against domination by the state, legally bound to increase profit. As corporations search for the lowest possible operating costs, they often resort to exploiting both humans and the environment. They use their financial power to lobby for more and more rights over communities and people. Poverty, loss of biodiversity, war, and environmental destruction have all been outcomes of this drive for profit.

The corporate world can be characterized as globally competitive, hierarchical in structure, product and consumer focused, exploitative of the Earth's resources and people, and, of course, profit-seeking on behalf of shareholders, who are investors in the corporation's capital.

Within the corporate world there are efforts to create businesses that are ethical. There are corporations producing products resourced responsibly, with employees who receive a living wage and are treated well in safe working conditions. There are corporations that report environmental, social, and community bottom lines as well as financial. Some do it to "greenwash" themselves so that consumers will buy their products believing that the corporation is environmentally or socially responsible. Others do it because they believe it is the only ethical way to run a business.

Unfortunately the majority of corporations operate in a way that is damaging to the environment and/or humans and/or communities. Current laws encourage publicly traded companies to ensure that profit for shareholders comes before all else. Let's look at some of the characteristics we describe above as a way of understanding how destructive practices occur in the corporate world.

Walk into your local stores and you will see products made in China, Taiwan, Japan, USA, Philippines, and India, to name a few.

Whether it is a car, cell phone, or ferry, there is a high likelihood that it was produced outside of North America. What you are witnessing is economic globalization, the international exchange of goods and services. There are a myriad of players involved in and impacted by economic globalization, along with a myriad of corresponding societal stories.

Story #1: Consumers

Some people have a positive story about economic globalization. They emphasize that, when products are produced in places where the cost of production is the cheapest, the end user pays the lowest price for the product. They describe the economic advantage of large quantities of a product being produced, enabling manufacturing efficiencies that lower the end price for the consumer. In order to sell large quantities, they argue that products need to be available internationally while being manufactured in countries where the costs are lowest. They believe trade barriers should be eliminated so that the free market can determine prices.

Story #2: Working conditions

People doing the work of manufacturing and producing products have different stories. For example, there are the many low-paid workers in countries with very few labor laws and regulations. Their story is about dangerous working conditions and subsistence wages that allow manufacturers to price their products low and still make a good profit. There are varied stories within this group of workers as, despite the conditions, they make more money than they would otherwise and thus can support their families. There are also workers in countries such as Canada or Germany that have substantially more regulatory support to ensure safe working conditions, and a higher minimum wage. However, there have been fewer and fewer manufacturing jobs for them as companies head to those countries with lower labor and environmental costs.

Story #3: Ecological systems

Ecological systems are impacted in numerous ways due to economic globalization. The environment has been damaged by resource extraction, livestock grazing, pollution from fossil fuel use in industrial operations, and the transport required to ship products from one part of the world to another. The damage to our ecological systems has not been factored into the cost of products and instead is considered an externality, or side effect. Some jurisdictions have started putting in life-cycle requirements for products produced in their country. Other countries have not. In a global economic market the implementation of this kind of initiative can result in companies that are not concerned about their environmental impact moving to countries without such strict and expensive regulations.

Story #4: Influence on the system

Consumers play a large role in influencing global economics. Their priorities when purchasing products contributes to determining what gets produced. If their priority is the lowest cost, without consideration or concern for environmental or labor impacts, then manufacturers and companies will find the lowest-cost locations. Those consumers who decide to buy only local or buy only products that have been produced under good working conditions, with minimal or no damage to ecological systems, can influence manufacturers to shift their practices. However, when enough consumers are primarily looking for the lowest price, then many manufacturers will decide to just produce products for those consumers and not change their poor labor or environmental practices.

Story #5: Global competition

Those manufacturing the products also have a story. To compete in the global market, manufacturers are drawn to countries with minimal labor and environmental regulations, lowering their costs and increasing their net profit. They are able to do this when consumers choose low prices over concern for negative impacts on the environment and workers. On the other hand some manufacturers may appeal to consumers concerned about the ecology and/or human rights. Their products are produced in an ecologically sustainable fashion, while at the same time maintaining high labor standards. Manufacturing by these companies is more likely to be found in countries with higher environmental and labor standards.

Story #6: Multinationals

Those multinationals that only care about the bottom line have the money required to influence decision makers and law makers in ways that further increase profit margins. Laws that have been put in place in recent years primarily stem from trade agreements. These laws give preference to the rights of corporations over the rights of individuals, communities, and governments. Corporations aimed at reducing cost go to countries with the lowest labor costs and lowest environmental standards. We can see this when we look at where our clothes, our shoes, our computers, and so many more products are made.

There are many more stories that could be told, and within each of the broad stories above are many diverse opinions.

So, outside of capitalism, what other types of economics are part of our world? In *The End of Capitalism as We Know It* Julie Graham and Katherine Gibson describe how non-paid housework, growing and gathering food, caring for children and elders, and volunteer labor are all forms of economy that are not capitalist. Re-use of waste, goods exchange such as clothes swaps or bartering systems, cooperatives, and paid labor not aimed at producing a profit are also outside of capitalist practices. As we start to add up the hours and efforts we discover that more hours of labor (over the life course of individuals) are spent in non-capitalist activity than in capitalist activity. The stories in the following pages take us into the non-capitalist practices that are flourishing, despite sitting in the midst of capitalist stories and systems.

Changemakers' Economic Stories

Getting off the treadmill

We met Rebecca earlier, in the food and shelter chapters. Rebecca, with her partner, Alex, decided to go a different route than their classmates after finishing their degrees: "We are ditching the dominant system which dictates that we should have a great big house that we go into massive debt to obtain."

Instead they lived in a yome (a hybrid between a yurt and geodesic dome) while building a house as eco friendly and sustainable as possible, within their budget. Rebecca reports, "We are building as we can afford it, mortgage free, using our own sweat, blood, and sometimes tears to get this done so that we can truly enjoy it when it's done." Their approach frees up time for "good scenery, good food, and good company. These are all things that we really, really value and try to include in our everyday life on a regular basis."

Egg of Wisdom

upon reflection   Their decision to "ditch the dominant system" speaks to their awareness of the dominant narrative and the potential for alternatives. Their choice also speaks to agency, their recognition that they have internal authority. They did not bow down to the cultural expectations expressed through mainstream media. They understand that there is more than one story about success—they don't have to buy the big house and incur massive debt; instead they have chosen a lifestyle that fits with their values.

While Robb took a different route than Rebecca and her partner, he was aware in his early twenties of the consumer culture aspect of the dominant narrative. After completing a physics degree, he realized that he could rent a $100-per-month cottage for six months, do some contract work, then head off traveling for the remainder of the year. In his late twenties he moved to one of the Gulf Islands, found inexpensive accommodation, and continued the pattern: "Six months on, six months off eventually evolved to the 20 hours a week which I do now." Robb's rejection of material status symbols, including a big house with a corresponding mortgage, allowed him to choose a lifestyle focused on enjoying life: "I'm not doing this for altruistic reasons; you know, I'm not going to live miserable just because it's understood to be 'the right thing to do'—I live as I do because I get great pleasure from it."

Rethinking work

There are many ways to rethink work. In the preceding stories we heard how Rebecca and Robb have described their personal approaches—less consumerism means less need to earn money. In this story we will hear how the Mudgirls Natural Building Collective has chosen a different organizational form for their work. Fay met with Rose, one of the members.

Rose describes how the collective is structured—"a consensus-run collective of individuals who choose to earn money as part of a collective." They create and refine their policies through a group process at the beginning and end of the season:

> We call them [the group processes] "boots on" and "boots off"—
> our own form of boot camp. (There is a lot of humor in the process—that's huge. That's possibly the key that holds it all together.)
> At the meetings we hash out our policies. We go over what worked and what didn't work, what all of our experiences have been, and who our clients have been. At every workshop we clarify at the beginning what our goals are.

The Mudgirls Collective decides who will work on specific jobs through what they call "the computer":

> Each year we update what our interests are, what our new skills are, and those all go into the computer—it's like a point system.

It's a system based on skills, location, willingness, whatever—but as we all become more skilled it's more difficult for the computer to figure out who should get any particular job. When the coordinator is hired then they figure out what skills are needed for each job and how many jobs there are, and then that gets posted and we all apply.

Different members of the collective take on different roles. Rose, the woman I spoke to, was the contact person for requests coming in from their internet site. Another woman is the "vibes watcher." Her role is to identify issues to address before they create problems among the Mudgirls or their workshop participants. Rose explains:

We sit in a circle and go over together what is going on.... Sometimes one person might be in a mood—you know, maybe feeling too rushed.... So it's not necessarily "You're a bitch," or whatever. Instead, what are the circumstances this person is dealing with? Are they feeling pressure from the client? Have certain things been said and are there hurt feelings? Say they're rushing everyone and then everyone is feeling it. That kind of stuff can happen. Once you just acknowledge it—it dissipates on its own to a large extent.

The importance the collective places on effective communications is evident in their requirement that everyone have some training in non-violent communication (also called compassionate or collaborative communication). Rose says, "We try, if a conflict comes up, if there's ever a small accident, or someone gets hurt, or there's an emotional issue...well, you know, we all try to be conscious communicators."

They recognize that even in their own group there may be good intent at cross purposes, and they have created a way to allow those experiencing different realities to understand each other and work effectively together.

When I asked Rose to clarify a comment she'd made on wealth hierarchy (see next story) related to other cob building workshops, she responded, "I don't have a ton of experience as I haven't actually been to those other workshops. So it's just how I've observed it, my sense of how it is." Her response demonstrates a principle of non-violent communication through her recognition that she can only speak from a place of experiential knowledge about what she has personally been involved in, and she can describe another situation in terms of observation but not from a place of truly knowing their story.

upon reflection The Mudgirls not only demonstrate how important it is that we allow multiple realities when we are working collaboratively but also how crucial it is to understand how to live with and respond to those multiple realities.

Wealth hierarchy

Rose's comment about wealth hierarchy was in reference to the way in which the Mudgirls charge for workshops (what they call work parties) relative to other natural-building organizations:

Something that we saw in the natural-building industry is that experts hold workshops and participants pay, say, a thousand dollars, and those participants are paying to build someone else's house. That's kind of confusing—why would a home owner have other people pay to build their house? Home owners are already landowners, so it's sort of a strange wealth hierarchy. These people that want to learn are working for you and paying to do so.

In the traditional approach to cob building workshops, the owners don't pay for their house to be built. Instead, workshop facilitators charge approximately $1,000; in exchange, they teach the participants through the hands-on work of building the owner's house. The owners don't have to pay for the labor that is provided by the participants, and the facilitators are paid through the participant fee.

That's a really common way to do it, but we don't do that. Our clients pay us—we keep our wages relatively low, but fair, enough for our own needs.

In the workshops put on by the Mudgirls the homeowner pays the Mudgirls' wages (as teachers/facilitators and builders). The fee that participants pay covers the cost of food, the cook's wages, and the child care. A different mode of thinking creates a different wealth distribution model and ensures that the work parties are affordable and accessible and that homeowners don't make money from those building their home.

There is also evidence of a different mode of thinking in their barter system, approach to child care, and emphasis on empowerment, just as their approach to workshop fees demonstrates their choice to exercise their free will.

They base their barter system on work carried out by members of the collective on the cob homes of other members of the collective, exchanging their labor in return for future labor on their own homes. Child care is an important component of the barter workshops and the work parties. Rose describes how child care is valued as an equal contribution to the building and facilitator roles:

Free Will

> There is a tendency in our culture for child care to be minimum wage, and we don't think that's fair—they make an equal contribution to the job being done. Without it we wouldn't be able to do the job. And we don't want strangers taking care of our children either, so we recognize that it's a really important job—it's a tremendous responsibility.

upon reflection The Mudgirls collective embodies the importance of thoughtful reflection, open communication, and continuous learning. The process of work—its organization and the way it is conceptualized—is central to the work they do, both for customers and for each other.

Room to grow

Shelagh moved to Hornby Island in 1969. There were about 150 people on Hornby at that time. She describes how Hornby Island residents expanded their school:

> When I first got to the island, the main school was a one-room schoolhouse, and the old one-room schoolhouse was next door. Dianne and I, in 1974, opened the old school as a preschool. The Hornby Island School was very crowded, and it was clear more space was needed. The case was made to the Department of Education, but they said it would take five years to build a new school. [The school only went up to Grade 7.]
>
> I was at a PTA [Parent Teacher Association] meeting, and we were sitting around talking about the immediate need, and although it looked like the community would get one eventually, it wouldn't help our kids. Tim Biggins said, "Let's just do it ourselves! We'll just build it and then we'll rent it to the school board."
>
> What we built was, technically speaking, a portable, since it was on posts. But it was a gorgeous building, designed by an architect, built by Hornby builders and volunteer labor—dozens of people worked on it. It was very funky and down home.
>
> We called it Room to Grow. Stevie Kittelson, a silversmith on the island, came up with the name. Not sure how we did it, but it belonged to the PTA, and we rented it to the school board. We were the richest PTA in BC! We made somewhere between $300 and $800 per month. We had a wonderful time. The kids went on trips, and we bought musical instruments and did all the things you could do with enough money.

What Tim did was create the Hornby Island Educational Society, which then became the official owner of Room to Grow. The rent received by the society went to the PTA for all of the activities, events, and instruments described by Shelagh. Shelagh notes, "Tim Biggins had been a member of the school board of a tiny school district in California that did this kind of thing on a regular basis."

Room to Grow is still owned by the Hornby Island Educational Society and is now the home to many classes and groups, such as life drawing, belly dance, ukulele lessons, youth dance, and Hornby's own fabulous quilters.

upon reflection   So many projects from Hornby Island are inspiring! Room to Grow, the Co-op, the Free Store and Recycling Center to name a few. Hornby has been an example of collaborative and collective practice in the Gulf Islands for many years. However, following Hornby's model of collaborative practice is carried out in ways that work for each community rather than being copied exactly; people everywhere have their own ideas of how to accomplish things in their own context, and that is as it should be. All of these groups taking action inspires others, though, and the "Let's do it ourselves" cry of Hornby finds its echo elsewhere.

Social enterprise

The corporate world has informal as well as legal systems to protect those making a profit. The air-to-air heat pump social enterprise described in the People Power chapter is part of the dominant wholesale purchasing and distributing system. However, the system is used not to make a profit but rather to provide an alternative for people and organizations to decrease their energy use.

A Nanaimo distributor responded to an article about the social enterprise by rallying together other distributors and attempting to get the wholesaler to dethrone Chris, the manager of the social enterprise, as a dealer. Their rationale—the social enterprise approach takes away business from those making a legitimate profit off the units. They used the fact that Chris was not a registered air conditioning refrigeration technician (a requirement for one component of the installation) to persuade the wholesaler that he shouldn't be a dealer.

Even though the wholesaler was making more profit from the social enterprise initiative (at that point the social enterprise dealership had sold 50 residential units compared to fewer than 20 from all the other British Columbia dealers combined), the wholesaler was concerned about offending the Nanaimo distributor. Chris negotiated with the wholesaler, and they agreed to move the dealership over to the company doing the refrigeration component of the installation, while still maintaining the social enterprise aspect of the initiative.

When told about the Nanaimo dealer's reaction and the final arrangement, Gary, one of the heat pump purchasers, indicated that he could understand the response from the other dealers. Chris had broken the informal agreement among the dealers that they would keep their mark-up prices around the same level so that all the dealers could make a good profit off the heat pump units. According to Gary, the dealers' approach was part of regular business practices and part of a healthy economy, and such practices need to be supported.

Gary's concerns reflect the dominant culture's belief about economic self-interest trumping environmental or social goals. The social enterprise reflects an ecological way of thinking, with Chris and others volunteering their time so that the heat pumps are affordable. As a result, more people are able to use them and reduce their energy use, thus reducing negative environmental impact and in the process reducing their monthly expenses. In 2012, the manufacturer informed Chris that he had "sold" more heat pumps than any other British Columbia dealer.

Transformative spaces

upon reflection   Stories about how business should be done, stories about economic self-interest, stories about attaining environmental or social goals through a social enterprise are all floating in the same space in this tale. How many people may have witnessed this transformative space and started questioning the mainstream way of understanding business, and how many could not accept there might be a different way of doing business?

Common stewardship

How can we shift from an ownership culture to a culture of the commons when the law is based on property ownership? The Gabriola Commons is one example. The Commons' story is told by Judith:

In the beginning there was no word for what was about to happen. In fact there was no clear beginning. Before the days of the Weldwood conflict, before Folklife Village, by the mid-'90s the island was growing, infused with vitality, and when the goat farm came on the market, it was obvious to think of it not only as beautiful land but as a home for a library, for the doctors' office, for the large home-schoolers group—there were over 300 in the group at one time, quite different from today—for PHC [People for a Healthy Community], which was then in a little place above Suzie's [a local restaurant], for an Islands Trust office [the local government], which had no space at the time, and for the arts group—which had been borrowing space at Camp Miriam for a long time.

In fact, it was recognized during the writing of the Official Community Plan (OCP) of the time that this parcel of land, the goat farm, was destined to become a non-commercial community space. This was written into the OCP. A group formed to consider making this happen, but the price tag was a little daunting.

Enter Amazing Grace Ecological Society (AGES). It was ten years later (in 2005), and they had a dream and enough capital to secure the down payment and to sustain mortgage payments for over three years. Heide and Shelagh [two of the three AGES board members] had the imagination and courage to welcome the community into a three-day forum, recognizing that their initial vision for the property might not be supported by all. They took a chance by saying, "What if no one wants to do what we've imagined happening? Well, okay, if they don't want it, we'll listen to what the community says." As it happened, the community response was extraordinary, generating a steering committee that was to meet bi-weekly for two and a half years to create what all could see was an unusual project.

upon reflection Some ideas keep coming back, circling towards birth, until the time is right. The community had identified this specific location as a potential community space in the OCP prior to the visioning session that took place in 2006. This cumulative process is consistent with a process described by many of the storytellers, a cyclical one always involving an idea that comes back around repeatedly.

The "time was right" for the Commons. When Jay Mussel, a long-time community activist and resident of Gabriola, knew he was dying, he arranged for his estate to be used to establish the Amazing Grace Ecological Society. The Society's purpose was clear but not tightly defined—essentially it was to do something good for the Earth.

spiral of change

The trustees recognized the great benefit the goat farm could convey to the community and took rapid action to purchase it when it came on the market, with money from Jay's estate. The trustees provided not just a down payment but also three years of funding to cover the mortgage costs. So, there was time for many conversations, with an initial visioning session to which everyone from the community was invited and all stories and ideas were welcomed. Out of this session, and based on ideas created through a continuing visioning process, a group formed to consider various options as to how the land could be owned by the community and accessible to all.

Shelagh had moved to Gabriola from Hornby. She had studied Elinor Ostrom's work on the effectiveness of Commons and introduced the concept of the Commons into the conversation. The steering group took a couple of years looking at various options, and the tools available, as well as the requirements of various government regulations, in order to determine how best to create a Commons. Three core elements that create the framework for the Gabriola Commons are the organizational structure, the local government by-laws, and the proposed covenant.

The organization is non-hierarchical and consensus based. There is a coordinating council and various teams that meet at the coordinating council to make joint decisions. There is a property-management team, a farm team, a sharing the Commons team, a trustees team, and several more. The trustees team is a charitable society and is the legal owner of the Gabriola Commons. All decisions are made by consensus.

The land was zoned single-family residential, so the trustees team needed to work with the Local Trust Committee to develop appropriate zoning so that the various community activities that were envisioned could be carried out on the property. Many of the concepts and activities did not fit easily into land-use zoning regulations, as Sheila, a former member of the LTC, describes:

> The idea is much bigger than a land-use by-law. Sometimes you need a space or a facility to enable those conversations. But transformation is never going to happen inside a regulatory zoning tool.

Deb, one of the original members of the Commons, was elected as a trustee (of Islands Trust, the local government) and struggled with the contradictions. Sheila reflects on Deb's struggle with those contradictions:

> I remember she drew this cartoon, when she was first a trustee, about this great big beautiful idea of the Commons and her as the trustee wrestling it in—kind of pounding it down with her copy of the Official Community Plan.

The process of creating a zoning by-law that allowed the majority of proposed activities to happen took a couple of years and substantial work on the part of community members and the Islands Trust planners.

The by-law went to public hearing, and changes were made as a result of input from the community, but in the end it was approved. One of the volunteers working on the by-law process with the Islands Trust was so frustrated and exhausted by the end of the process she stopped volunteering at the Commons. However, Judith did not even mention the by-law process; instead she focused on the community process of creating a space that moved away from land ownership and moved towards stewardship, in the spirit of those who lived on the island before colonization. Her story was about the system-change aspects of the Commons, not the regulatory issues.

A covenant document has been created and is now being reviewed by a retired eco-justice lawyer volunteering his time to ensure it is airtight from a legal perspective. The document lays out the principles, philosophy, governance, and ecological protection for the 26-acre piece of land. The Covenant team will then take the document to potential covenant holders, who will be responsible for monitoring the activities and ecology of the Commons to ensure that the Gabriola Commons remains true to its principles and philosophy.

Not-for-profit products

Living simply and buying less is at the heart of many of the personal stories. However, we still need to eat, cook, dress ourselves, keep our shelters warm, keep clean, and other activities that require things. There are ways of acquiring things that can be just, healthy, and ecologically responsible.

In this book we have heard about both sources and products that fall into that category—free stores, heat pumps, biodiesel, Lulu's Local, Cable Bay Farm, and Glean soap. The not-for-profit products are out there—we just need to see it as a treasure hunt with a cornucopia of surprises awaiting us.

Cooperatives

Cooperatives are a tool to shift our economics from competitive to cooperative, from individualistic consumerism to a sharing economy, from profit for shareholders to profit that can be funneled back into the cooperative or provide dividends to the cooperative members.

Financial cooperatives

We were united about the types of innovation that should happen.
—CORO STRANDBERG

A group of socially progressive directors were elected onto the
VanCity Credit Union Board of directors in the mid-1980s, and
they brought a sea change that has influenced other credit unions
and corporations across the world. Coro Strandberg was one of
those directors. Coro describes how the group transitioned the
business model of the credit union from the mid-1980s to the
mid-1990s:

> *We were all interested in social innovation. The decade included
> prototypes and pilots to test out ideas. We didn't have a road-
> map. We didn't know that we were transforming the business
> model at the time. We were testing ideas, and we were united in
> the direction we were going.*

What types of innovation did they test out? They created the
Vancity Community Foundation, a model based on community
development rather than philanthropy. As Coro describes it,

> *The mission of the Foundation was to act as a catalyst for the
> growth and empowerment of disadvantaged groups and com-
> munities served by Vancity through providing loans, technical
> assistance, or funds for community economic development and
> housing alternatives.*

Another leading-edge pilot the group initiated was Vancity Enterprises, which provided "affordable housing through innovative
development strategies involving community groups, churches,
and governments."

This innovative board of directors initiated the idea of social
accounting in 1990. In his annual report, the chair of the board,
Bob Williams, listed the various social innovations Vancity had
achieved, including a lending program for women working at
home, a peer lending program through the community founda-

tion, the creation of the Enviro Fund Visa Card (a percentage of revenue going to environmental initiatives), a loan to a Sikh organization for a community center, and a new Vancity branch with 34 apartment units on the top floors for single parents.

Vancity has been the leader in many of the current accepted progressive financial practices. They were the first financial institution in North America to provide loans to women with no male co-signer and the first to offer a daily-interest savings account. They were the first in Canada to offer Ethical Mutual Funds (the Ethical Growth Fund), the first to establish a branchless bank, and the first to market to the gay and lesbian community through mainstream media. They are also the first financial institution to attain carbon neutrality. Their social accounting, turned triple bottom line (people-planet-profit), turned Integrated Report, has been on the leading edge of reporting since that small group of passionate and innovative directors were elected in the mid-1980s. Their practices spread through the living net and are now being implemented in financial institutions across North America.

Coro describes how Tamara Vrooman (the current CEO) has taken all of the successful prototypes and pilots, created during two decades of social innovation, and solidified them into an internationally recognized progressive organization. In the past two years Vancity was named Canada's Top Corporate Citizen, Canada's Best Employer,

Living Net

as having the Best Integrated Report, and as one of the world's Top 25 For-Benefit Companies. In 2016 Vancity provided $18.5 million to members and communities. That's 30 percent of their 2016 net profits. A far cry from 1983, when Vancity provided $60,000 to communities based on a philanthropic ideology. Today VanCity is the largest Credit Union in Canada, with 523,000 members, 59 branches, and $19.8 billion in assets.

Vehicle cooperatives

My rationale for joining the carsharing co-op in Nanaimo, and then serving on the board for several years, was primarily to save money by eliminating the need to take a car on the ferry to Nanaimo for most errands. As the years went by, the environmental plus of carsharing began to catch on.... It was rewarding to be part of an emerging social trend. [John]

John was a board member of a carshare cooperative that recently joined the MODO Carshare Cooperative. MODO is located in the cities and suburbs of Vancouver, Victoria, and Nanaimo. When the Vancouver-based cooperative started in 1997, it was the first carshare in the English-speaking world. Like many other co-ops, Modo started with passion and an innovative idea. Tracey Axelsson, the person who initiated the Cooperative Auto Network (later to become MODO), drew her inspiration from a model in Germany. In 1995 a friend showed her a three-minute video clip of a carshare cooperative in Cologne Germany, and the spark was ignited.

She based her master's thesis on the idea and applied for grants to get it started. She received $20,000 from VanCity Credit Union and another $20,000 from the Cooperators Insurance Company, and she, with others, were on their way to establishing the first carshare co-op in North America.

Two decades later there are over 18,000 members, 800 businesses, 100 building developers, and several local municipalities that use MODO. There are also carshare cooperatives throughout Canada and the United States. For those interested in starting one up in their community, Transition United States has posted a "How to Start a Car-sharing Cooperative" article on its website.

Cooperative stores

The Hornby Island Cooperative store was established in 1955. Today, $110 provides you with a membership and a share in the store. Doug tells the story: "It's called a co-op store and that's exactly what it is. People donated funds and then also loaned funds, and they went ahead and did it." It is also a gathering place, "the core of Hornby Island—we all meet each other at the store." The shares are investments, used for upgrades and maintenance, with any profit made returned to the members based on their patronage. Members also vote on the management of the store.

upon reflection   Whether it's Vancity, with $19.8 billion in assets, or the Hornby Island cooperative store, these enterprises are owned by those who use the services. The profits don't flow to distant stockholders, and the decision making is democratic and driven by the needs of those using the service rather than those wanting a good return on their investment.

To ponder

Reflect on your community. What are the primary economic exchanges in your community, your region, or your country? Are there formal cooperatives in your community? Are there informal cooperatives or collective approaches to work, to business, or to providing services? What actions have people and businesses taken to shift their exchanges to local relationship-based exchanges rather than long-distance corporate exchanges? How are the learning and knowledge about different forms of economic exchanges being transferred within your community, as well as between your community and others across the continent and beyond? How have your personal economic habits shifted as you learned different stories about economics through compassion, wisdom, and practice?

From Analysis to Activism

Moving towards change

Stories don't end when the story is over. The stories of things that have happened to us, or that we've taken part in, can still have an influence even when we think they are long forgotten. They can change us, our community, and our world in a way that doesn't stop when they do—or even when we do. By changing ourselves, we change the world.

All the stories we've shared in this book are stories of change. Sometimes the change is in a community. The story of Gertie the bus is the tale of a group of people who looked around and said, "Why can't our small island have a bus?" From further afield, the story of the banning of plastic bags in Concord, Massachusetts, is a community story that began with one boy talking to his grandmother about plastic bags and the damage they can do to the environment. Sometimes the change is less in a community than it is in an individual—Leah, for example, suddenly noticing all the factors there are to consider in buying, well, just about anything.

But by changing ourselves or changing a relatively small detail of the way we live we change the world. By our transformation, we make the transformation of others more likely because we have changed the conditions in our community/location.

There has been criticism of this kind of argument recently. Various opinion pieces in respectable sources have told us that individual change won't eliminate climate change or solve other problems. Instead, what we need are sweeping systemic changes and, in particular, changes to the function of corporations and senior levels of government. So why do we remain convinced of the value of individual transformation as a way of saving the world?

We see the beginning of change as occurring within individuals, because there is nowhere else for it to happen. Groups *per se* don't suddenly change their practices—it is groups of individuals who do this, whether it's a family or a neighborhood association or any other organization. Governments don't change laws and legislation without individual change happening first. Someone thinks something was a good idea, convinces others of it, and then legislative change can occur, almost always following rather than leading citizens. Elected representatives may not be passionate supporters of everything they support, but they certainly do recognize when their constituents support change in sufficient strength to have an impact on subsequent elections. Corporate change can be seen the same way. Companies change their policies and practices when it becomes more difficult and less profitable to stay the same than it is to change; that happens when individuals in large numbers, at the level of customers and at the level of shareholders, make profit-seeking in the old way much more difficult. At the heart of every change there is individual learning—an individual changing his or her mind.

And we do see hope in the kind of change we are talking about—changes begun by determined individuals and small groups have expanded well beyond that group. Think back to Anna and her egg. Since the time of that story, access to local food has expanded considerably in our local community. The Agi Hall farmers market welcomes farmers from several organic farms, and two other new markets also operate on the island. Each year brings more roadside stands. The local supermarket now has a prominently labelled local food section in the produce depart-ment, and more local products throughout the store. This isn't all Anna's doing, of course—her actions joined with an up-swell of interest in local food—yet her story helped draw attention to what was possible.

We see hope in the story of Gertie the bus, too. The volunteer-initiated and -managed community bus has been running on Gabriola for five years now. Other communities have been in touch to learn how to build a similar system, and there's a network of community bus groups planning a Bus Love-In to share infor-mation and work towards changing some of the regulations that are designed for much larger systems.

And we find hope beyond our own community, too, in actions taken in the past and those building for the future. We find the bodhisattvas of wisdom, compassion, and practice everywhere.

Manjushri

Over fifty years ago, for example, American biologist Rachel Car-son's book *Silent Spring* alerted the world to the dangers of pesti-cides and their accumulation in the food chain. Her work helped to launch the modern environmental movement and contributed to the rise of organic farming. She warned that public officials were too ready to listen to the claims of profit-motivated industry and, in the estimation of many of her readers, made it almost im-possible to dismiss environmental pollution as "just the price of progress"—at least, not without an argument. Carson is a classic bringer of wisdom in the style of Manjushri. In her case the flam-ing sword was her research in marine biology and her eloquent writing voice.

Avalokiteśvara

Today, entering a modern building in Canada or the United States using a wheelchair or another mobility device, the disabled ex-pect to have the same access as anyone else. Fifty years ago, this level of accessibility was almost impossible to imagine. The right to this access is enshrined in law—in the Americans with Disabilities Act (ADA) in the USA and various pieces of legislation in Canada. This is not attributable to any one individual. Disability rights movement historian Arlene Mayerson explains:

> The history of the ADA did not begin on July 26, 1990, at the signing ceremony at the White House. The ADA story began a long time ago in cities and towns throughout the United States, when people with disabilities began to challenge societal barriers that excluded them from their communities, and when the parents of children with disabilities began to fight against the exclusion and segregation of their children. It began with the establishment of local groups to advocate for the rights of people with disabilities. It began with the establishment of the independent living movement, which challenged the notion that people with disabilities needed to be institutionalized, and which fought for and provided services for people with disabilities, enabling them to more easily live in the community.
>
> The ADA owes its birthright not to any one person, or any few, but to many thousands of people.

Thousands of people—thousands of eyes and ears to see and hear what is needed, and arms and minds to work for change. In this example, we see a reflection of the compassion of Avalokiteśvara, acting from a passion for justice.

Samantabhadra

In 2015, the Truth and Reconciliation Commission of Canada released its final report. The Commission spent six years traveling throughout Canada, hearing from Aborginal people who had been forced as children into residential schools. The report is beautifully written—and difficult reading. It reports the experiences of almost 6,000 witnesses, the survivors of a school system that was designed to support the practice of cultural genocide. The report documents the experiences of children who were abused, traumatized, and ill-treated in all imaginable ways. It begins,

> *Canada's residential school system for Aboriginal children was an education system in name only for much of its existence. These residential schools were created for the purpose of separating Aboriginal children from their families, in order to minimize and weaken family ties and cultural linkages, and to indoctrinate children into a new culture—the culture of the legally dominant Euro-Christian Canadian society.*

The title of the report, *Honouring the Truth, Reconciling for the Future*, carries the clear intent to be more than a document about a devastating past. Since the publication of the report, Canadians have been talking about reconciliation and what it means.

Against this background, Gord Downie, famous in Canada as the former lead writer and singer for the rock band The Tragically Hip, took action. He created a multimedia project *The Secret Path*, sharing the story of 12-year-old Chanie Wenjack, who died of starvation, and exposure in his attempt to flee a residential school in winter. In 2016, with Chanie Wenjack's sister Pearl by his side, Downie debuted the songs and film at a concert in Ottawa. Soon after, the Assembly of First Nations honored him in an emotional ceremony. According to a CBC report, "Newfoundland, Labrador, and Nova Scotia Regional Chief Morley Googoo said Downie was a living embodiment of the push to reconcile relations between Indigenous and non-Indigenous peoples."

The work of being a living embodiment is the work of Samantabahdra, inspiring others to take the difficult steps needed for reconciliation between the Aboriginal and non-Aboriginal population.

These stories have not ended. The work of reconciliation between Canada and Aboriginal First Nations has barely begun. Disabled people's access to buildings is enshrined in building codes, but in both Canada and the United States those with disabilities earn only two thirds to three quarters as much as those without current disabilities. DDT has been banned for agricultural use worldwide since the 2001 Stockholm Convention on Persistent Organic Pollutants, but the challenge of protecting people from chemical and other pollutants continues.

Change is not easy. We are not likely to transform together in an easy walk towards some perfect endpoint, when the planet will be safe and all our difficulties will be resolved. The stories we've included in this book often show the complexities of even seemingly simple issues and the ways in which different people can hold very different perspectives on the same event. What strikes us, though, is the sense of energy and happiness people bring to their work for change.

From the practical to the personal

Since change must, by definition, involve individual change, it is practical to think about from this perspective. But this too is more complex than it might first appear.

The kind of change we are talking about in this book—the stories that we have shared—reflects a strong connection between individual actions and personal values. Again and again we heard people describe how the actions they took and the changes they made developed from their values. At times, we heard how those changes, once made, encouraged people to look even more closely at their own values, and perhaps make further changes. We have a strong sense of a circular kind of process. Someone's personal values push them to look at the way they do something in their lives. They make a change to bring that part of their life into closer alignment with their values. Once they've done that, they realize that the change itself prompts them to further consider some other aspect of their values, and so on.

This might sound like a grim and somewhat arduous process, but for most people it doesn't feel grim. There is something deeply satisfying about reflecting on the way we are in the world, and that's what we're doing when we think about the connection between our values and our everyday actions. There's something even more satisfying about living a life that is deeply aligned with our values. This could be one definition of happiness.

Happiness is not to be underestimated, since we seem to be living in a time of increasing despair. Climate change is a growing reality, and we are beginning to see its impact. The world political situation seems dire, with record numbers of people forced from their homes as refugees, whether by war, politics, or famine. There is so much we can point to. It is easy to feel that there is absolutely nothing that we as individuals can do—and yet, if anything is to be done, it will be done by individuals. Working towards a positive change engages us and is a powerful antidote to despair. When some of what we do is focused on our own very local actions, we are able to see real progress and change. This perspective can help keep us engaged for the long haul and help us to overcome our sense of personal despair.

We are each at the center of a circle. We have (within reason!) complete control over the events at the center of the circle, in the sense that we decide our personal actions. The choices we make are influenced and formed by our life experience and our interaction with others, yet we have free will and do make choices. As we move further out in the circle, our influence is lessened. We have influence on our family, slightly less on our immediate community, and less still as we move further from the center.

That doesn't mean that we have no influence beyond the immediate. What it does mean is that our attempts to influence change beyond the immediate might be less obviously successful than our efforts to make changes in our own lives. We need to remember the living net metaphor, with many threads taking local actions and spreading them further and further. We might be aware of some of those threads and their resulting actions, but for the most part we are not. Yet change is happening.

Going forth and working on those broader changes, in a way that is grounded in our own values and the changes we have made in our own lives, may not provide us with immediate concrete evidence of change. But if we understand the concept of the living net then we can embrace hope and, by working with others to make those broader changes, recognize that there is an invisible impact to those actions.

Using learning to move towards change

The three metaphors for learning have great strength as a tool for analyzing situations where change might be valuable. As we look upon a difficult situation, we can ask ourselves questions based on these approaches to learning. These questions can really be quite simple:

+ What wisdom can be brought to bear here?
+ Is there an available example of a different way of doing things?
+ What are the struggles/feelings of those in this situation—those who are committed to staying the same as well as those who are committed to change?

Asking these three questions encourages us to maintain an attitude of curiosity. We find, as we walk around issues with these questions in mind, that we're able to move away a little from a tendency to hurry towards a solution. The questions help us move from analysis towards a kind of grounded activism—from "What is the reality of this situation?" to "What can I do about this situation/what changes can I make in my life to be more consistent with my values?" to "What changes can we as a community make?"

We found ourselves making this kind of shift as we reflected on the stories in the process of writing this book. Some of our reflections ended up as a consideration of next steps—wondering what the people involved in the story could do next. Others left us wondering "Who else?"—what other group or community could benefit from this example? These kinds of reflections show some of the ways that exploring from the basis of what has been learned, or what could be learned, helps us move from individual action to the broader circle of community.

But what about Really Big Change—transformation in governments and transformation in social systems? Although systems themselves are large, sometimes global in scope, the process of change still begins with the personal and the local. Change that seems to an observer to begin at the outer sphere (a change instituted by a level of government, for example) really doesn't—individuals elsewhere have changed first. This doesn't mean that no major change can happen until absolutely everyone who might feel its impact has changed. We're convinced, though, that efforts towards individual change, and change in our local communities, are the starting point.

In the next chapter, we'll take the next step, helping you to explore how these ideas could work in your own community.

Changemakers' Manual

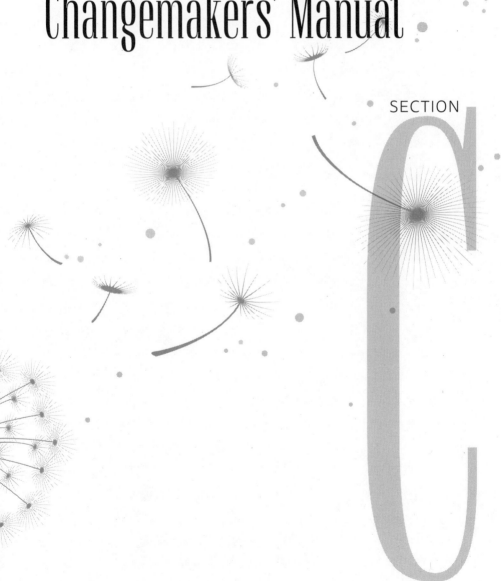

Introduction

As we've been writing this book, exploring the stories of change and thinking about what they mean for us and for the world, we've also been thinking about how they can be useful—how they can inspire more change. This chapter is one response. It is a hands-on workshop for those who want to build change. There may be a need in your community that you want to respond to, or you may have already started implementing a change initiative. This chapter helps you walk through the steps to turn that idea into reality.

We've been imagining you reading this—someone who sees the need for great or small changes in society and has made, or is in the process of making, change in your own life. This chapter is designed to help you move the process of change out through your sphere of influence—from you as an individual through your household to your community and beyond. With Margaret Mead, we are convinced that small groups of committed people can change the world. This chapter will help you and your small group do that.

We've spent a lot of time thinking about you and all the possible circumstances where you might find yourself. Perhaps, like us, you live in a small community with a strong tradition of citizens doing things for themselves. Perhaps you live in a big city, in a neighborhood where people are concerned about some aspect

155

of civic life. Perhaps you are part of a group that is already concerned about the world—a faith-based group, a union, a parents' organization, or a blockwatch program. Perhaps you are an activist, committed to social change and looking for ways to encourage others to share your concerns and build your community. And perhaps you are living in a tiny, isolated community, where change seems unlikely and your sphere of influence feels particularly small.

You and your group may already have a particular concern in mind, or you may be motivated by a more general desire to Do Something about the many problems you see around you. Or perhaps you don't actually see yourself as part of a group working for change—perhaps it is just you, reading and wondering what you might do about some of the situations you see.

We've referenced the stories in this book throughout the manual. Reading and working with the stories lets you explore the central ideas in this book with real examples. The stories can be an excellent opening for conversation—first about the stories themselves and then about the situation you are thinking about in your own community. You may find it useful to spend more, or less, time on the stories, depending on you or your group.

Whatever your circumstance, we hope this practical, hands-on guide will be useful for you.

Using this manual

This chapter supports different ways that you can bring people together—in ones or twos, in small groups, or larger groups—to have the kinds of conversations that lead to practical work for change. It provides multiple approaches and techniques you can use to facilitate meetings, workshops, or short courses in a wide variety of settings.

Because we can't know everyone's circumstances, we've designed this workbook section to provide flexibility and choices. We've included

+ A suggested plan for using the ideas in this book as a basis for talking about change in your community. The plan describes a

step-by-step approach to a series of seven gatherings, including detailed instructions for a facilitator. It provides options,
so whether your group is you and your next-door neighbor or
a larger gathering, you should find value here. You can follow
this plan with or without a facilitator, depending upon what
works for your group.

+ A collection of activities and approaches based on our many
  years as group facilitators and participants. We hope you will
  find some useful ideas here, whether you intend to use our
  plan or do something different.

We've included a section called "Facilitation techniques," at the
end of the seven sessions, to describe some techniques in more
detail.

The plan is divided into seven sessions.

+ Session One: Transformative Spaces
+ Session Two: Learning Change
+ Session Three: The Genesis of Ideas
+ Session Four: From Spark to Action
+ Session Five: Cross Purposes and Spirals
+ Session Six: Linking with other Changemakers
+ Session Seven: Societal Change

Let's begin...

SESSION 1
Transformative Spaces

How do people change and develop the stories that guide them in the world? How do we create transformative spaces? What is the link between stories and action? What is the relationship between agency and hope?

Key points
+ Integrity and values
+ Different stories and multiple realities
+ Transformative spaces
+ Letting go
+ Free will and agency

[I] = one or two people; [S] = small group; [L] = large group

---

+ Integrity and Values

Read: A Tale of Egg and Agency, p. 3

Guiding question: What values does Anna hold that lead to her actions?

Provocative question: Imagine the health inspector asking Anna for $100 for her to receive a "special" permit (wink, wink). What do you think Anna would have done?

Activity: Each participant selects photos that represent the intersection of their everyday life and values. Think about [I] or describe in group [S] or [L]. How do these values relate to the community initiative you are considering or the need you want to respond to?

Note: Spread a collection of images on a table. (Magazines are a good source.) Works best if there are at 10–20 images per person to choose from.

• Different Stories and multiple realities

Probing question: What are the different stories in Egg and Agency?

Activity: Divide into teams for each of the stories that the group identifies. Have small-group discussion, then each team explains what their story is and explains how their values inform their story.

Note: For example, one customer's story might be the story of a young parent who wants to purchase the best possible food for their child—they need to talk about how their values will determine whether they listen to the inspector or to Anna.

• Transformative Spaces

Framing: Personal transformation starts with being in a space that offers opportunities for us to hear new stories about ourselves and the world around us.

Activity: Have a moment of silence while participants think about the preceding sentence in relationship to "the egg" story as well as their own ideas and initiatives. Then open up for discussion: Who in the story might shift to another story? Are there times in your life when you have been in a transformative space? Have there been transformative spaces related to your community idea or initiative?

✦ Letting Go

Framing: If Anna were going to shift to the inspector's story, what would she have to let go of? What would the inspector have to let go of?

Guiding question: Think about your own life—can you describe a shift in story that required you or someone else to let go of a belief attached to an initial story?

Note: This could lead to a discussion of your community initiative; what will you be asking people in the community to let go of?

✦ Free will and Agency

Framing: Diagram plus explanation, which includes Anna's values and her actions = free will (choice) + agency (actions)

Activity: Participants draw their own big circle and little circles based on an experience they have had regarding stepping outside the dominant story's circle. Those willing to share describe the different stories, their choice, values, and actions.

Check out/debrief: Bring closure to the session. Choose a closing activity from the suggestions in the Facilitation Techniques section or something else that works for you and the group.

SESSION 2
Learning Change

How can critical reflection, compassion, and mindful practice teach us new practices and approaches?

Key points
- Critical reflection
- Compassion
- Mindful practice
- Learning as interconnection

✦ Critical Reflection

Read: Rebecca's story in Changemakers' Shelter Stories (p. 61)

Guiding question: In Canada and the United States, new houses average about 200 square meters (2,200 sq ft). What might inspire someone like Rebecca to build a much smaller house with natural materials?

Provocative question: How would your community be different if everyone lived in a small house? A large house?

Activity: Working together (or in groups of 3 or 4 for larger groups) create a mind map with "the shelter" at the center. Encourage people to think about what shelter means and how it connects to other aspects of life.
   Post the mind map(s) for reference.

Note: Shelter is used throughout this session as an example, to introduce and practice working with the tools. If your group is working on a specific issue, use shelter as a quick mind-map example; analyze the map (next step); then do a mind map with your issue; and work through the session in detail.

✦ Compassion

Framing question: What do you think of when you hear the word "compassion"? Are there ways in which compassion seems to be relevant to Rebecca's choice?

Activity/discussion: Look at the connections on the mind map. Ask: "With the connections I've made, am I/are we bringing compassion to this topic? Am I/are we bringing critical thinking to this topic?"

Examining questions will likely reveal the interconnections between critical reflection and compassion.

✦ Mindful Practice

Framing: We're engaged in mindful practice when we are doing things in a way that is consciously in alignment with our values.

Activity: In pairs, talk about something you do that is consciously aligned with a deeply held value. Have you always done it that way? If not, what prompted you to change?

✦ Learning as Interconnection

Framing: Critical thinking and compassion often go hand in hand, and exploring them helps us identify and apply our values.

Guiding question (for groups thinking about a specific issue or solution): Have we looked at our community need or initiative plan from the perspective of compassion and critical thinking? What values are we demonstrating in practice as we work on this initiative?

Check out/debrief: Bring closure to the session. Choose a closing activity from the suggestions in the Facilitation Techniques section or something else that works for you and the group.

SESSION 3

The Genesis of Ideas

How do you move from concern through analysis to a plan for change?

Key points
+ Dissonance and resonance
+ Ways of learning: critical reflection, compassion, mindful action
+ Gathering information: dreaming of possibilities
+ Connecting with others
+ The "how" of change

Read: Artists and soap-sellers, p. 51

[I] = one or two people; [S] = small group; [L] = large group

---

✦ Dissonance and Resonance

Guiding questions: Read Leah's story in the Food chapter (p. 47). How does her story reflect dissonance and resonance?

Provocative question: Does anyone ever get "it" all sorted out, so that there is only resonance and no dissonance?

✦ Ways of Learning

Framing: Critical reflection, compassion, and mindful action (especially looking for examples) are ways to generate ideas, as well as ways to thoroughly examine ideas and situations that create dissonance/resonance.

Activity (Think, Pair, Share, see p. 180):

Think: Think back to Leah's story of buying, or not, local honey. Remember her questions around money versus supporting the local economy. On your own, think of a situation (a product purchase or an action) where you experience a similar conflict.

Pair: With friends [I] or a partner [S & L], consider these questions about your situations:

+ If we bring critical thinking to this issue, what actions might we take to resolve the dissonance?

+ If we bring compassion to this, what actions might we take to resolve the dissonance?

+ Thinking of mindful practice, can we think of someone who seems to have resolved this issue?

Share: Your experiences and anything of particular note (not all conversations.)

Note: Participants' stories may not be closely connected to the initiative you are planning or the need you are addressing. The purpose of this activity, and the one that follows, is to explore a way of looking at situations deeply and from multiple perspectives.

+ Gathering Information

Framing (mini case study or quick brainstorm): Imagine that you live in a community with only one grocery store. Very little local food is available there. To purchase food that is locally grown, you must drive approximately 30 minutes on a busy highway. Because of your concern about climate change, you are not happy with either option. *How could you gather information to help you choose an option or find a new path?*

Analyzing your situation: Apply the same brainstorming approach to one or more of the situations that participants identified earlier.

◆ Connecting With Others

Roundtable sharing: Using a talking stick or other means of controlling air time, each person shares the information-gathering idea they heard that they would most like to pursue.

Note: Information-gathering ideas will focus on the specific need or initiative your group is working on.

◆ The "How" of Change

Working together: Those with similar interests group together and plan next steps.

Activity: Check out/debrief

SESSION 4

From Spark to Action

How do ideas go from spark to action? In this session, we will describe those initial steps that a small group of concerned citizens take as they start to turn an idea into reality.

Key points

+ What's the need?
+ A small group of concerned citizens
+ Develop a plan
+ Research
+ Start moving forward

Read: The Gertie bus service, p. 84

[I] = one or two people; [S] = small group; [L] = large group

---

✦ What's the Need?

Guiding questions: What need was identified that resulted in Gertie? What other needs might have been identified that would have resulted in a bus? Were there other solutions to the need?

Activity: In small groups (3–4) each person in the group describes the community need they have identified and the solution identified for the need. Others in the group then come up with other potential solutions and also identify other needs that respond to the proposed solution.

Activity: Brainstorm different activities to reduce community GHG emissions (or to address the need the group is focused on); then vote using dotocracy—see p. 180.

✦ Becoming a Group of Concerned Citizens

Activity: Either individually or in small groups write down/ discuss the different steps that occurred in the Gertie story, from the initial conversation in the kitchen to the group gathering to organize fund raising and the pilot. Now describe the steps you have taken or plan to take with your initiative.

Guiding questions: A community meeting to gauge interest was one of the first steps—what came out of the meeting? Are there other ways to get community direction in the early stages?

Are there other ways to find other "concerned citizens" who are willing to work on the initiative?

Framing: Culture of the organizing group is crucial. A key element that worked for Gertie was inclusivity. People felt they had a voice about how to move forward, both within the group and in the community.

Activity: Brainstorm different inclusivity strategies (i.e., non-hierarchical, public outreach) then divide into groups [L] or pairs [S] and give each group/pair one of the strategies. Using their own change projects, they then discuss how they could implement that strategy. If [I] then identify how each strategy could be used for your initiative.

✦ Develop a Plan

Activity: If [L] divide into small groups to work on your initiative. If you have already received community input, work with the next steps identified. If you have not, what next steps do you think your community would propose?. Develop the plan based on those steps—give a sense of time and who might work on each specific action.

Guiding discussion: What came up in your group as you were creating the plan? Did the culture of the group support the work or get in the way?

Note: This planning process can bring new ideas and approaches to light, even if the group has already developed a specific plan for an initiative.

✦ Research

Framing: Finding out what other people have done about a need, what people in your community think about the need, what funding might be needed, and what resources are available to help you are all key pieces of information that are invaluable when working on a community-change action.

Activity: Take your community initiative and start identifying what you would need to know and how you could go about getting that information. Add it to the plan.

✦ Start Moving Forward

Guiding question: What do you need to consider when deciding how your group will be organized?

Activity: Brainstorm structures and processes for organizing: Organizational structures (registered society, informal, charity), internal structure (non-hierarchical, hierarchical, a combo), decision-making (consensus, voting, combo), etc.

Activity: Identify three different change projects. Participants choose their favorite choice of structure for each change project using dotocracy.

Provocative question: You now have a plan and an organizing group, but these aren't the most important keys to turning a spark into reality. What do you think are the keys? (The authors believe passion is one of the keys but are open to other opinions.)

Activity: Each participant talks about something they are passionate about [I, S], or participants pair up and share with each other [L].

Activity: Debrief/check out

SESSION 5

Cross Purposes and Spirals

You're moving forward and then "screeech," something slows you down or stops you altogether. Usually a cross purpose is the culprit. In this session we will explore how to respond, how to keep going, and how to know when the time is right to launch your change project.

Key points

+ Cross purposes
+ Understanding and addressing
+ Moving forward
+ Just do it—the time is right
+ Spiral

Reading: Mudgirls Natural Building Collective (p. 63) and Fueled by waste vegetable oil (p. 101)

[I] = one or two people; [S] = small group; [L] = large group

---

+ Cross Purposes

Guiding questions: So, you are humming (or bumbling) along, moving forward on your plan, and then you bump up against someone (or an organization) that stands in the way of achieving your change. What stood in the way of getting insurance in the Mudgirls' story? What were the different stories in the same space? What was the purpose behind the insurance company's list, and who were the beneficiaries? What about the Mudgirls and their client?

Activity: Break up into three groups. First group focuses on regulatory cross purposes, second on "good" purposes but different priorities or values, and the third on personal

---

cross-purposes (need to own, need to direct others, etc.). Come up with different examples from your own experiences.

✦ Understand and Address

Activity: Stay in the same groups. Take each of your examples and describe the rationale and beneficiary for each cross purpose. Then discuss strategies to address each one.

Report back: Each group uses two examples to demonstrate the source, rationale, beneficiary, and your suggested strategies to address them. Open up to the rest of the groups to discuss strategies and whether there are other suggestions.

✦ Move Forward (*The fun part!!*)

Framing: It is possible to get discouraged when cross-purposes interrupt your moving-forward flow. This is often the time when initiatives halt or wind down rather than moving forward.

Activity: Brainstorm a list of strategies that would help a team move forward. Add "celebrate successes" to the list if it isn't there. Do something celebratory (a round of applause for everyone getting over the "cross-purposes" hump—or whatever works for your group).

✦ Just Do It—The Time is Right

Framing: Community buy-in is crucial to a project succeeding. While not everyone will always agree, there does need to be enough support to make it work.

Guiding question: What were the signs in some of the stories we've read so far that indicated that the community was ready? For projects that you've worked on or are currently working on, what were/are the signs?

Guiding question: Outside of community buy-in, what are some of the other factors that might need to be in place for your initiatives?

Activity: Take the community initiative you are working on and identify what is needed to launch it. Break into pairs [S & L]. Each person presents their initiative and describes what is needed to launch it to the other person. For [I] discuss with friend. Get feedback regarding how to move forward on those aspects not in place yet.

✦ Spiral

Framing: It took two years before the egg regulations were changed. It took five years before Gertie was launched. Most projects spiral towards a time that is right.

Activity: Each participant takes a big sheet of paper and draws a spiral. They choose a story (from the book or their own change project) and start at the large end of the spiral and write the different events that occur along the way. Put in cross-purpose points, community engagement successes, and whatever else just feels right! Share the spirals.

Activity: Check out/debrief

SESSION 6
Linking with Other Changemakers

Change ideas spread as demonstrated by the neighborhood affect. In this session we explore how the living net comes to life as ideas and challenges are shared and collaboration between changemakers creates broader change.

Key points
+ Living net
+ Neighborhood effect
+ Sharing ideas and challenges
+ Collaborating on broader changes

Read: Energy audit lending library, p. 110, and Heat pump social enterprise, p. 112.

[I] = one or two people; [S] = small group; [L] = large group

---

+ Living Net

Framing: So your idea is now a reality. There have already been some threads and nodes shifting in the living net as you work towards that reality. Let's find those transformative spaces in the stories we've discussed so far.

Activity: Participants take spiral sheets from Session 5 and put colored notations in the places they believe might have been transformative spaces. Discuss whose story might have shifted and what kinds of actions might have happened as a result.

Activity: Draw threads at the end of the spiral, and write down who might be influenced after the launch.

✦ Neighbor Effect

Framing: Research into solar power in Connecticut demonstrated what researchers called a "neighbor effect": a change made by some inspires others to make the same change.

Guiding question: In what way did the heat pump initiative demonstrate the "neighbor effect"? What about some of the other stories we've read?

Activity: Share in pairs [S & L] or write down your thoughts [I]. Think about a group you are part of—it could be your neighborhood or it could be an online group focused on a particular activity or interest. Was any change made that inspired others in the group to make the same change? Why?

Note: This kind of change reflects the importance of mindful practice and learning from the example of others.

✦ Sharing ideas and challenges

Guiding question: Kim provides us with a clear example of how ideas can be shared—from individual to group to community and then from community to community. Can you think of times when you were the sharer of an idea? Times you were the recipient of an idea?

Activity: Break into small groups [L]. Each person shares an idea they have put into action. (It can be individual change or group change.) Group members ask questions about the idea.

Guiding question: How many asked questions about the challenges? Why is it important to share the challenges with the ideas?

◆ Collaborating

Guiding question: Are you aware of any nearby communities that have individuals or groups interested in similar ideas? Have you connected with them?

Activity: In groups of three identify an idea that one of you is working towards, and put that in the center of a flipchart page. Put other points on the page that represent people or groups that you could work with on your initiative—whether it is about sharing solutions to challenges or changing regulations. Draw a line from your idea to the other ideas. On the line describe what you could achieve with that collaboration.

Activity: Debrief/check out

Homework activity: Research the different groups you've identified and look for other groups that might be relevant to your idea. Bring the research to Session 7.

SESSION 7
Societal Change

How can we draw connections between local change and societal change? How can we expand the influence of our change work?

Key points
+ Globalization and local spaces
+ Accumulations of localisms
+ Shifting stories
+ Societal change

[I] = one or two people; [S] = small group; [L] = large group

---

+ Globalization & Local Spaces

Framing (making connections): In our interconnected world, most actions have a direct connection to distant parts of the world. Think of the project you are working on. In what ways does it connect to places far away? (Prompt to think about supplies, news of the project spreading, etc.)

+ Accumulation of Localisms

Activity: Sharing news from other nodes.

Read: The story sections in From Analysis to Activism, p. 143—the stories of increasing availability of local food, the expanding influence of Gertie the bus, stories about Rachel Carson, of disabled individuals' access to buildings, and of Gord Downie and his work in reconciliation.

First, share stories you are familiar with of times when individual or local action had influence beyond the local.

Second, share examples of other communities that are trying to do similar things to your project, or that somehow are logical to link to. Refer to the research you did between sessions, when you identified other groups your initiative might connect to.

Note: This activity may require some individual research prior to gathering.

◆ Shifting stories

Activity: Spheres of influence. Draw a representation of spheres of influence (a series of concentric rings, with "you" in the middle, then family, community, region, etc.)

As a group, consider your project. Where is it located on the sphere of influence diagram? Is it located in the same place for each of you? How might it be relevant for the next circle out? How can you, as a group or individuals, enhance its impact there? Beyond that ring and even further?

◆ Societal Change

Activity: Dream big. Working independently, reflect on what *could* happen if your project is successful beyond your community—and beyond your wildest dreams.

To conclude the activity, share this Henry David Thoreau quote: "If you have built castles in the air, your work need not be lost; that is where they should be. Now put the foundations under them."

Note: Depending on your group, participants might enjoy sketching their idea, writing a brief reflection, imagining a broadcast news report.... Encourage imagination.

◆ Next Steps

This is up to you and the group!

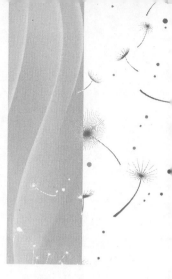

Facilitation Techniques

Discussions

Techniques are designed to make sure everyone is heard from and that one or two people do not do all the talking.

Talking stick: Bring an object like a stick, ball, or something else large enough to be visible around the discussion circle. Each person holds the object while they speak; no one is allowed to speak if they do not have the talking stick.

Chips or pennies: Give each person a number of pennies, poker chips, or similar objects. Each time anyone makes a contribution to the discussion, they put their penny in a jar. When they are out of pennies, they cannot speak again until the next discussion.

Preliminary reflection: Before you pose the discussion question, tell participants that they will have one minute of silence to think about it before discussion begins. Time the silence—it may seem long! (Quick moves into discussion tend to favor extroverts, who are often happy to work out their ideas by talking about them. Introverts tend to like to think about things first, then present their idea.)

Think/pair/share: Give participants a brief amount of time to consider their response to a question or idea. Then pair participants and ask them to discuss their responses together. Finally, call on pairs to share the main points they discussed. (With a large group, you may not have time to call on every pair.)

Summary build: Ask each person to summarize and respond to something said by the speaker before them, then add their own point. ("Keisha, you said that the new schedule should make it easier for parents to attend meetings. I agree, and I think it might also be helpful if we provided activities for older children. And I also wonder if we could...") This encourages participants to listen to each other rather than waiting for someone to finish while they plan their own next statement.

Yes/no brainstorm debate: Present the proposal or position. Explain that everyone will speak in response to it, to say either yes or no and provide a reason. The trick is that yes and no responses alternate—if it's your turn to speak and it's the turn of a "no," you need to say no and come up with a reason, even if it isn't what you actually think. (This is a useful way to explore possible opposition to an idea or position the group unanimously agrees with.)

Dotocracy (sticky-dot voting)

Use dotocracy to identify group priorities for future action.

+ Display the group's ideas. These will often have come from a brainstorming session and may be recorded on a flipchart or whiteboard. As much as possible they should be easily accessible (for example, on a wall with space in front of it) and easy to read.
+ Give each participant a certain number of sticky dots (typically 3–5).
+ Ask participants to place their dots beside the idea that is most interesting to them, or the question they feel is most important to address, the issue they think the group should tackle next—whatever priority determination is needed.

- The technique works best if participants place only one dot beside each action they think is important rather than putting all their dots in one place.

Brainstorming Techniques

It can be helpful to set rules for brainstorming—ideas only, not critique.

In brainstorming, groups tend to come up with more diverse ideas if they begin by brainstorming independently. They come up with more (but more similar) ideas if all brainstorming is done together.

Sticky note groups

Give participants several sticky notes large enough for writing a sentence or two. Participants write their ideas in silence. Once ideas are written, gather the group around a flipchart stand, or a large piece of paper mounted on the wall. Ask one person to place one of their notes on the wall and read it to the group. Then ask if anyone else has something similar (same idea, related to the same aspect of the topic, etc.). If so, get them to place and read. Once similar ideas are placed, move on to the next idea. Ask the group to create headings for each of the idea groups. (This gives everyone credit for thinking of the most common ideas—typically the quickest speakers come up with them first—and helps build group respect.)

Six Thinking Hats

Edward de Bono developed the Six Thinking Hats technique for structured brainstorming. Explain how it works to participants before you begin. Ideally everyone should think with each of the hats. (That is, everyone should identify emotions, facts, positives, negatives, etc.) Use it as follows:

- Identify an issue. For example, lots of traffic near a school.
- Blue hat—What is our goal? For example, make it safer... make it less noisy...make it less damaging to the climate... (Note that these can include big-picture ideas.)

+ White hat—Facts: What information is available? What needs to be found? (What time of day...statistics on number of cars...)
+ Red hat—Emotions (no justification needed). (For example, this makes me angry...this scares me...negative or positive emotions...)
+ Black—Discernment: Why should we be cautious about taking action or making this choice/decision? (Parents are going to be angry if we tell them not to drive...lots of people commute using this route, so speed bumps will cause disruptions...)
+ Yellow—Optimism. (We can improve the atmosphere around the school...working together on this problem will help bring the community together...)
+ Green hat—Creativity: Thinking outside the box to solve the problem. (Could we have a walking school bus for drop-offs? Car-pooling?)

Mind Map

A visual tool for brainstorming that encourages participants to draw connections between their own ideas (when done individually) or others' ideas (when done together). There are many variations on mind-mapping; this is one simple approach for an individual mind-map.

+ Write a concept in the center of a large piece of paper (for example, shelter).
+ Somewhere else on the page, write down an idea the concept brings to mind (for example, house). Connect the concept to the idea with a line.
+ Does the idea "house" generate further ideas? Add them. (For example, "house" might generate ideas like "family" "comfort" "debt" "work"...) Connect them with lines in a way that seems logical to you.
+ Note: If you're doing this with a group, you need a large piece of paper and the ability to write quickly! Practice with a small group first to decide what's practical for you.

Checkouts/debriefs

Close each session with a short debrief. This gives you a chance to see how the session went and helps you make necessary adjustments for the next session.

There are lots of ways to do this. Here are some possibilities.

+ Ask participants to write a one-minute paper, writing what they found most interesting about the discussions that day.
+ Ask participants to speak in turn, identifying either something they learned through the course of the session or something they are still wondering about. Make note of the things that are still being wondered about, and check to be sure they will be addressed in an upcoming session, if appropriate.
+ Collectively, make a list of ideas you want to consider in future sessions or things that don't quite fit so far. These can be kept in a "parking lot"—a list on a flipchart page is convenient for this—and brought along to the sessions. Revisit the list from time to time to see if there are things that can be addressed now or that should be removed.
+ Ask participants to think about the discussion and then respond to four one-word prompts: What do you plan to Start, Stop, Continue and/or Change based on our work here? (Many participants won't have responses to all the prompts. To share, ask them to identify one of their responses—don't expect four).
+ Put a line on a whiteboard or flipchart page to divide it in half. On one half, write "Worked well." On the other, write, "Do differently." Give participants sticky notes. Ask them to write their (anonymous) comments on the notes, and add them to the appropriate section.
+ Next steps: Is the group engaged in planning an immediate project? If so, it is useful to dedicate some time at every meeting to thinking about practical next steps. The kind of deep planning for change being done in these sessions is valuable; there's also an additional component of specific, practical planning that is required.

+ Be prepared to change. You may find that participants in your group don't like some kinds of activities, or don't see the value of particular conversations. Be prepared to explain why you think they are important, and also be prepared to change your plans. Developing your small, committed group of people to change the world is more important than following a particular process.

References

America's Electric Cooperatives (2017). *America's Electric Cooperatives 2017—A Fact Sheet.* Retrieved from electric.coop/electric-cooperative-fact-sheet/.

Bakan, J. (2004). *The Corporation: The Pathological Pursuit of Profit and Power.* New York: Free Press.

British Columbia Egg Marketing Board (2011). *Egg Industry in British Columbia.* Retrieved from bcegg.com/files/egg-industry.php.

Canada Food Inspection Agency (2011). Egg grading. *Food: Eggs and Egg Products.* Retrieved from inspection.gc.ca/english/fssa/concen/specif/eggclae.shtml.

CanEquity (2012, January 19). Canadian homes growing in size, becoming less affordable. *CanEquity News and Blog.* Retrieved from canequity.com/news/6240-canadian-homes-growing-in-size-becoming-less-affordable.

Carroll, W. K. (1997). Social movements and counterhegemony: Canadian contexts and social theories. In W. K. Carroll (ed.), *Organizing Dissent: Contemporary Social Movements in Theory and Practice* (2nd ed., pp. 3–38). Toronto: Garamond Press.

Castree, N. (2004). Differential geographies: Place, indigenous rights, and "local" resources. *Political Geography, 23,* 133–167.

Castells, M. (2012). *Networks of Outrage and Hope.* Malden, MA: Polity Press.

Chandler, A. (2016) Why Americans lead the world in food waste. *The Atlantic,* June 15, 2016. Retrieved from theatlantic.com/business/archive/2016/07/american-food-waste/491513/.

Cohen, L. (1992). *First we take Manhattan.* Retrieved from leonardcohen.com/us/music/im-your-man/first-we-take-manhattan.

Gabriola Commons Foundation. (2011). *Constitution.* Retrieved from gabriolacommons.ca/pdf/constitutionbylaws2011.pdf.

Gooch, M. V., and A. Felfel (2014). "27 billion" revisited: The cost of Canada's annual food waste. Value Chain Management Centre. Retrieved from vcm-international.com/wp-content/uploads/2014/12/Food-Waste-in-Canada-27-Billion-Revisited-Dec-10-2014.pdf.

Davis, M. (2006). *The Planet of Slums.* London: Verso.

De Schutter, O. (2010). *Report Submitted by the Special Rapporteur on the Right to Food*. Commissioned by the United Nations General Assembly, December 20, 2010.

Deffeyes, K. (2005). It's the end of oil. *Time International* (Canada Edition), 166(18), 38–38.

Dermody, J. (2011). Consumerism. In J. Mansvelt, and P. Robbins (eds.), *Green Consumerism: An A-to-Z Guide*. (pp. 86–89). Thousand Oaks, CA: SAGE Publications, Inc. doi: 10.4135/9781412973809.n32.

Downey, L., E. Bonds, and K. Clark (2010). Natural resource extraction, armed violence, and environmental degradation. *Organization & Environment, 23*, 417–445. doi:10.1177/1086026610385903.

Eigg Electric (2017). *Eigg Electric*. Retrieved from isleofeigg.org /eigg-electric/.

Environment and Climate Change Canada (2017). *Greenhouse Gas Emissions from the Transportation Sector*. Retrieved from ec.gc.ca /indicateurs-indicators/default.asp?lang=en&n=F60DB708-1.

Food and Agriculture Organization of the United Nations (2009). *The state of Food Security in the World: Economic Crises—Impacts and Lessons Learned*. Retrieved from fao.org/docrep/012/i0876e /i0876e00.htm.

Food Banks Canada (2016). *Hunger Count 2016*. Retrieved from foodbankscanada.ca/documents/HungerCount2016_web.pdf.

Foucault, M. (1982). Is It Really Important to Think? An interview translated by Thomas Keenan. *Philosophy and Social Criticism*, 30–40.

Gabriola Health Care Society (2010). *Results of the Gabriola Island Health and Well Being Survey*. Victoria: Vancouver Island Health Authority.

Galbraith, K. (1996). *The Good Society: The Humane Agenda*. New York: Houghton Mifflin Company.

Gibson-Graham, J. K. (1996). *The End of Capitalism (As We Knew It)*. Cambridge: Blackwell Publishers Ltd.

Gottshall, J. (2012). *The Storytelling Animal: How Stories Make Us Human*. New York: Houghton Mifflin Harcourt Publishing.

Gulf Islands Driftwood (2011, October 19). *Velo Village 2012: A Q & A with John Rowlandson*. BC Local News. Retrieved from bclocalnews .com/community/132119513.html?mobile=true.

Hansen, J. (2012, May 9). Game Over for the Planet. *New York Times*, p. A29.

Harvey, D. (2012). Rebel Cities. London: Verso.

Hawken, P. (2007). *Blessed Unrest*. New York: Viking Press.

Hsieh, Esther (2014). *She Quit her Job and Started a Car Sharing Company.* Retrieved fromtheglobeandmail.com/report-on-business/small-business/sb-managing/a-car-sharing-pioneer-before-there-was-car2go/article21301387/.

Home Protection Office (2008). *Report of the Green Roof Task Group.* Retrieved from hpo.bc.ca/printpdf/green-roofs.

Hornby Island Community Economic Enhancement Corporation (2007). *Housing Solutions for Small Communities Conference: Conference Report.* Hornby Island.

Hornby Island Recycling Committee (2009). History. *Hornby Recyclables.* Retrieved from hirra.ca/recycle/.

Intergovernmental Panel on Climate Change (2008). *IPCC Fourth Assessment Report: Climate Change 2007.* Geneva: IPCC.

Institute for Intercultural Studies (2017). *Frequently Asked Questions About Mead/Bateson.* Retrieved from interculturalstudies.org/faq.html.

Isin, E. (2002). *Being Political: Genealogies of Citizenship.* Minneapolis: University of Minnesota Press.

Isle of Eigg Heritage Trust (2017). *Isle of Eigg Heritage Trust.* Retrieved from isleofeigg.org/ieht/.

Jackson, M. G. (2008). *Transformative Learning for a New World View: Learning To Think Differently.* New York: Palgrave MacMillan.

Lennox, A. (2010). *The Story of Stuff.* New York: Free Press.

Lessing, Doris (1969). *The Four-Gated City.* London: MacGibbon and Kee.

Magnusson, W. (1997). Globalization, Movements, and the Decentred State. In W. K. Carroll (ed.), *Organizing dissent* (2nd ed., pp. 94–113). Toronto: Garamond Press.

Magnusson, W. (2003). Commentary on the Universal and the Particular: Sovereignty and the Urban Global. In W. Magnusson, and K. Shaw (eds.), *A Political Space: Reading the Global Through Clayoquot Sound* (pp. 113–120). Minneapolis: University of Minnesota Press.

Magnusson, W. (2011). *Politics of Urban: Seeing Like a City.* New York: Routledge.

Mason, B. (2008, June 23). Anna Bauer and the Gabriola Egg Stand. *Gabriola Sounder,* p. 1.

Massey, D. (2005). *For Space.* London: Sage Publications.

MacNair, E. (2004). *A Baseline Assessment of Food Security in British Columbia's Capital Region.* Victoria: Capital Region Food and Agricultural Initiatives Round Table.

Mezirow, J., and E. W. Taylor (2009). *Transformative Learning in Practice: Insights from Community, Workplace, and Higher Education*. San Francisco: Jossey Bass.

M'Gonigle, R. M., and J. Starke (2006). *Planet U: Sustaining the World, Reinventing the University*. Gabriola Island, BC: New Society Publishers.

Milner, G., WhyDev (2013). Don't Be Clothes-minded: Understanding the Impact of Donated Clothes. Retrieved from whydev.org/dont-be -clothes-minded-understanding-the-impact-of-donated-clothes/.

Ministry of Environment (2007). *Environmental Trends in British Columbia: 2007*. Retrieved from env.gov.bc.ca/soe/et07/04_climate _change/technical_paper/climate_change.pdf.

Ministry of Environment (2012). Ozone Depleting Substances and Other Halocarbons Regulation. *Industrial Waste*. Retrieved from env.gov.bc.ca/epd/industrial/regs/ozone/index.htm.

MODO (2017). *What's MODO?* Retrieved from modo.coop.

Natural Resources Canada (2017). *Energy Fact Book 2016–2017*. Retrieved from nrcan.gc.ca/sites/www.nrcan.gc.ca/files/energy/pdf /EnergyFactBook_2016_17_En.pdf.

Ostry, A., C. Miewald, and R. Beveridge (2012). *Climate Change and Food Security in British Columbia: White Paper*. Victoria, BC, Canada: Pacific Institute for climate change Solutions.

Polanyi, K. (2002). Excerpt from the Great Transformation (1957). In N. W. Biggart (ed.), *Economic Sociology* (pp. 38–62). Malden: Blackwell Publishing.

Priggen, E. (producer), L. Fox (director) (2007). *The Story of Stuff* [documentary]. Available from storyofstuff.org/movies-all/story -of-stuff/.

Rose, N. (2000). Governing Liberty. In R. Ericson and N. Stehr (eds.), *Governing Modern Societies* (pp. 141–176). Toronto: University of Toronto Press.

Sanderson, K., M. Gertler, D. Martz, and R. Mahabir (2005). *Farmer's Markets in North America: A Literature Review*. Saskatoon: Community-University Institute for Social Research.

Sinha, S. (2010). Dialogue as a Site of Transformative Possibility. *Studies in Philosophy and Education, 29*, 459–475. DOI 10.1007/s11217 -010-9189-4.

Solomon, S., D. Qin, M. Manning, Z. Chen, M. Marquis, K. B. Avery, M. Tignor, and H. L. Miller (2007). *Climate Change 2007: The Physical Science Basis*. Contribution of Working Group I to the *Fourth*

Assessment Report of the Intergovernmental Panel on Climate Change, Cambridge University Press.

Smith, A., and J. B. McKinnon (2007). *The 100-Mile Diet: A Year of Local Eating*. Toronto: Random House Canada.

Smith, D. E. (1974). The social construction of documentary reality. *Sociological Inquiry*, 44(4), 257–268.

T'Sou-ke Nation (2017). *Sun Keeps Shining on T'Sou-ke*. Retrieved from tsoukenation.com.

United States Census Bureau (2011). Median and Average Square Feet of Floor Area in New Single-Family Houses Completed by Location. Retrieved from census.gov/const/C25Ann/sftotalmedavgsqft.pdf.

van Loon, J. (2006). Network. *Theory, Culture & Society*, 23(2–3), 307–322.

Vancouver Island Community Research Alliance (2011). *Local Food Project: Strategies for Increasing Local Food Security on Vancouver Island*. Victoria: Office of Community Based Research, University of Victoria.

Vannini, P., and J. Taggart (2012, June 14). Outsmarting the meter: Off the grid on Lasqueti. *The Tyee*. Retrieved from thetyee.ca/Life /2012/06/14/Living-Off-the-Grid-On-Lasqueti/.

Vieten, C., T. Amorok, and M. M. Schlitz (2006). *I to we: The role of consciousness transformation in compassion and altruism*. Zygon, 41(4), 915–931.

Walker, D. (2009, February 17). When is produce safe to buy? *Nanaimo Daily News*. Retrieved from canada.com/nanaimodailynews/news /story.html?id=9d940872-2751-44d9-8ecb-be288e5b127a.

Wharf-Higgins, J., and F. Weller (2012). Citizen Participation in Social Policy. In A. Westhue and B. Wharf (eds.), *Canadian Social Policy* (5th ed.).

Zehner, O. (2012). Alternatives to Alternative Energy. *Bulletin of the Atomic Scientists*, 68, 1–7, doi:10.1177/0096340212459037.

Index

About the Authors

FAY WELLER is a community organizer, homesteader, researcher, and artist. She has focused on broad systemic change in her work and activism, and holds a PhD focused on social transformation. She is engaged in numerous collaborative initiatives from a local bus service to sustainability planning to affordable, low-impact heating. She nurtures, grows, and sells apples, eggs, and vegetables, and creates clothing from handmade fabrics. Fay has two adult children and a granddaughter. She and her partner, Bob, live with Yu and Mi, their two sheep, and numerous chickens on their farm on Gabriola Island, BC, Canada.

MARY WILSON has a longstanding interest in learning and communication for social change. She has worked for two decades as a facilitator, instructor, researcher, and instructional designer, and holds a PhD in education. As a student of Buddhism, Mary is fascinated by the Bodhisatvas—metaphorical enlightened beings who embody wisdom, compassion, and practice. She sees the combination of wisdom, compassion, and practice as central to learning and central to our collective efforts to live in harmony on our finite planet. Mary lives with her partner, her 93-year-old mother, and several critters on Gabriola Island, BC, Canada.

ABOUT NEW SOCIETY PUBLISHERS

New Society Publishers is an activist, solutions-oriented publisher focused on publishing books for a world of change. Our books offer tips, tools, and insights from leading experts in sustainable building, homesteading, climate change, environment, conscientious commerce, renewable energy, and more—positive solutions for troubled times.

We're proud to hold to the highest environmental and social standards of any publisher in North America. This is why some of our books might cost a little more. We think it's worth it!

- We print all our books in North America, never overseas

- All our books are printed on 100% **post-consumer recycled paper**, processed chlorine-free, with low-VOC vegetable-based inks (since 2002)

- Our corporate structure is an innovative employee shareholder agreement, so we're one-third employee-owned (since 2015)

- We're carbon neutral (since 2006)

- We're certified as a B Corporation (since 2016)

At New Society Publishers, we care deeply about *what* we publish—but also about *how* we do business.

New Society Publishers
ENVIRONMENTAL BENEFITS STATEMENT

For every 5,000 books printed, New Society saves the following resources:[1]

21	Trees
1,911	Pounds of Solid Waste
2,103	Gallons of Water
2,742	Kilowatt Hours of Electricity
3,474	Pounds of Greenhouse Gases
15	Pounds of HAPs, VOCs, and AOX Combined
5	Cubic Yards of Landfill Space

---

[1] Environmental benefits are calculated based on research done by the Environmental Defense Fund and other members of the Paper Task Force who study the environmental impacts of the paper industry.

Certified
B Corporation

MIX
Paper from responsible sources
FSC www.fsc.org
FSC® C016245

new society
PUBLISHERS
www.newsociety.com